God Bless —
Sandy

RESCUED

BY PRAYER

Twenty-four true stories of amazing answers to prayer

By

Sandy Ourso

ISBN 1-60034-434-8

www.xulonpress.com

Contents

Every story in this book is true.
Some names were changed and various incidental
facts were altered in order to protect
the privacy of certain individuals.

*This book
is dedicated
to
Lynn
and
Caroline*

*Special Thanks
to*

Kelly Alexander

Seafarers, the Concord and Caroline

Only be careful, and watch yourselves closely, so that you do not forget
the things your eyes have seen or let them slip from your heart as long
as you live. Teach them to your children and to their children after them.
(Deuteronomy 4:9 NIV)

Flying the Concord was one of the most amazing experiences of
my life. I have a background in art, and my artist's eye receives
great pleasure from looking at what I consider to be beautiful
airplanes. I think the Concord is the most beautiful of all. It reminds
me of a graceful crane when it lands, slowly floating toward the
ground, all white with its neck curved and its wings extended. It's
hard to believe that something so elegant could fly so fast. At Mach
II, it only took three hours to travel from London Heathrow to New
York's Kennedy Airport. It may not be an F16, but it's probably as
close as someone like me will ever come.

I vividly remember the physical sensation of being pushed back against my seat when the pilot kicked it up to 1,340 mph as we climbed toward 60,000 feet. I looked out the window and was shocked to realize that I could actually discern the curvature of the earth. I remember thinking about all the ancient seafarers who sailed the oceans, erroneously assuming that the earth was flat. I thought about how frightened they must have been, constantly watching, always worried that they would career over the edge, like going over some giant waterfall, crashing to their death into the nothingness below. I thought about how much I would like to write them a letter and send it back in time and tell them what I was seeing through the window of the Concord. "Rejoice!" I would say. "The earth is not flat. You're not going to sail off the edge." How relieved they would be, having leapt so far ahead of the normal learning curve.

Unlike those early seafarers who thought the earth was flat, my daughter knows that the earth is round. So that's one thing I don't need to tell her. But, like all parents, I've experienced a whole lot of other stuff she doesn't know. If I could hook her up to electrodes and shoot all of these great life lessons into her brain, she would be so far ahead of the normal learning curve.

At the date of this writing, no one, to my knowledge, has figured out how to do that. The next best way I know of is to *tell* her what I've learned.

The problem with the *"telling"* method is that she's a teenager. If I approach her with a conversation about any subject that is not of particular interest to her, and if she suspects that I might be planning to speak more than three sentences about that subject, her eyes roll back in her head and she begins to rock back and forth on her heels until I fear that she will surely crash to the floor out of sheer boredom.

Based on her reaction, I have cleverly deduced that she is not exactly clamoring for my sage advice. But I believe that God still expects me to find a way to teach her some of the more important lessons I've learned about Him – particularly about how He has rescued me in times of need. I believe that because of something He said to the Israelites.

When God was giving Moses instructions regarding the consecration of the firstborn, He said, "In the days to come, when your son asks you, 'What does this mean?' say to him, 'With a mighty hand the Lord brought us out of Egypt, out of the land of slavery.'" (Exodus 13:14 NIV) He wants us to tell our children, when they ask, about how He delivered us.

At the risk of being repetitive (another thing my daughter hates), we're dealing with the teenage boredom factor here. Caroline is not going to ask me what things mean. She's afraid she'll trigger a response that will require more than three sentences, thus keeping her away from the computer or the TV or her iPod or her cell phone for a potentially excruciating five minutes.

The wandering Israelites didn't have to compete with electronics. The only entertainment their kids had was throwing sand at one another. It would have been so much easier to get, and keep, the kids' attention if the kids weren't obsessed with how many people on their Buddy List might be on line at any given moment.

I still think God expects us to find a way. As it turns out, I stumbled on my way quite by accident.

My daughter is a voracious reader. She is drawn to the printed word like a clean baby to a mud puddle. She's one of those people who, like me, will read the back of the cereal box if nothing else is available. Coincidentally, I'm a writer. So, one day after I had written an article that I thought she would find amusing, I decided to put it on her bed to see whether she would read it. When she came home from school that afternoon, she went to her room and immediately read the article. She brought it back to me, smiled, handed it to me and said, "That was good, Mom," as she headed for the computer to Instant Message eight people at a time. Her eyes didn't roll back in her head, and she didn't rock back and forth on her heels.

It was one of the most significant "ah ha" moments of my life – when one of the great mysteries of the universe was suddenly solved, and my course of action became clear. I continued my experiment. About once a week, I would leave something on her bed. Like magic, she would stay in her room for a few minutes, reading the article, and then she would bring it back to me. It was a miracle! Not only was she absorbing the information I wanted her to have, but

I was able to present it in a much more thoughtful, organized way than if I had felt the pressure of having to quickly blurt out three sentences before she became catatonic.

So, I continued to write to Caroline about things God has done for me. At some point, I reread some of the articles and realized that a theme had begun to emerge. The theme was answered prayer.

And that, my dear reader, is how this book came to be.

My goal for this book, in addition to serving as an inspiration for Caroline, is twofold. First of all, I want to inspire you to partner with God in a way that will allow you to personally experience the power of prayer. Having God come through for you in answer to your prayer, no matter how small the rescue might be, builds intimacy with God in a way that few other things can.

Secondly, I hope you're inspired to write your own experiences for your children to someday read. What a legacy for your children and grandchildren – a journal of the times God rescued you from harm's way. It's wonderful for children to read about the times God rescued Abraham, Isaac, Jacob and all the other heroes of our faith. But few stories will touch a child in the same way as the stories of how God has manifested Himself in the lives of their very own family members. It is fabulous for kids to know about Moses and the burning bush. But, I promise you, they will be even more engaged when Papa tells them about the time the Lord rescued him when the bank was about to foreclose on the farm.

I hope you enjoy reading about some of the times God rescued me, or someone close to me, through answered prayer. And I urge you to begin making notes about your experiences. We need to teach our kids that the earth is round and other relevant facts. But the most important lesson you'll ever teach your children, and their children, is that generations of their family have called on God – and that He has been their strong and mighty fortress in time of need. Then they'll know that, like those before them, they can run to Him. They'll know that He will rescue them, too.

Chapter 1

I Was Blind, But Now I See

And ye shall know the truth, and the truth shall make you free.
(John 8:32)

And Isaiah boldly says, "I was found by those who did not seek me; I revealed myself to those who did not ask for me." (Romans 10:20 NIV)

Life was so much fun!

I know that stories of dramatic personal conversion don't usually start out that way. Sudden, miraculous conversions tend to occur when people are at the end of their rope, dangling precariously above the horns of some potentially devastating dilemma, with no choice except to turn to God and cry out for His help. All I know is that it didn't work that way for me. I was having the time of my life.

I had moved to Dallas in 1969, a time when companies were expanding and hiring almost any young college graduate who confidently sashayed through the door waving their degree and expressing an eagerness to begin their climb to the top. There was plenty of money for new projects, and no one had to worry about annoying cost cuts or about having to pinch pennies on their liberal expense accounts. Luxury apartments, extravagant homes and major highways were being built so rapidly that the landscape of this central Texas metropolis was barely recognizable from one year to the next.

When I arrived in Dallas, I had no children and no debt. I went to work at a well-paying job that I liked, and was able to spend my free time doing anything and everything that I enjoyed. Life was filled with travel, fine restaurants, season tickets for the theater, concerts, movies, shopping, and partying with friends. Raises came quickly, and my husband and I eventually remodeled a charming old red brick split-level near White Rock Lake, just a few miles from downtown Dallas.

One of the things I enjoyed in my spare time was reading. I had been a voracious reader since I learned how, and had a personal library that reflected my wide range of interests. My obsession with the truth tended to lead me toward non-fiction. I liked to find out things like why lightning sometimes goes from ground to sky, how to make a better pasta sauce, and what motivated Gandhi. My interest also extended to religions.

But I would never have regarded my interest in religions as a search for God. My mother had made sure that my three sisters and I went to church every Sunday when I was very young. But when I turned 15, I refused to endure the boredom any longer. I eventually came to sincerely believe that religion was simply a crutch for people who were too weak to deal with the hand life had dealt them. I didn't see anything wrong with that, mind you. I thought everyone who needed a crutch should have one. I just didn't happen to need one.

So, March of 1977 found me content and living the good life. If asked about my position on God, I would have selected the word "agnostic." I thought that was the appropriate word to reflect the blasé attitude of someone who was as sophisticated as I was beginning to feel now that I was living the good life in the big city.

Then something happened.

On March 22, 1977, I read a lengthy interview in "The Dallas Morning News" with a man named Francis Schaeffer. I had never heard of Francis Schaeffer. According to the article, he was a former Presbyterian minister who had left the organized church in order to establish a retreat in Switzerland called L'Abri. Dr. Schaeffer, who had earned a PhD in philosophy as well as a ThD, said in this article that he had founded L'Abri as a place for young people to search for answers. He didn't say search for God. He said search for answers. The article discussed Dr. Schaeffer's latest book, "How Should We Then Live – The Rise and Decline of Western Thought and Culture."

Schaeffer sounded like my kind of guy. He was obviously a brilliant man. And based on the fact that he had left the traditional church, I assumed that he was thumbing his nose at the establishment and offering shocking alternatives. I always found that intriguing. Although I led a traditional, productive life five days a week, my confused alter ego occasionally found expression as a weekend hippie. Saturday nights often found me at concerts, listening to groups like my favorite, Jimi Hendrix. I sometimes spent Sundays at Lee Park with my friends – barefoot, dressed in indecently short cutoffs, a halter-top and a fringed leather vest. I was a frequent defender of those who were downtrodden by "the man," and sympathetic with anyone who was bucking "the establishment." My friends and I advocated such causes as the release of Stoney Burns, controversial editor of "The Dallas Notes," the premier underground newspaper in the city. Burns had been sentenced to a long prison term for possession of a small amount of marijuana. We were, of course, convinced that "the man" was just trying to shut him up.

Looking back on all of that, I think the biggest favor anyone could have done for me in the early '70s would have been to lock me up on weekends. I take comfort in the fact that there were a lot of other people in their 20s during that period of time who were equally affluent, egotistical, misguided and vocal. Talk about a dangerous combination.

Anyway, Francis Schaeffer just struck me as the kind of guy who would have agreed with me on a number of issues – including the fact that Stoney Burns shouldn't spend 20 years in prison. So I went to the bookstore to buy his book.

As I was paying for the book, the clerk told me that Dr. Schaeffer was scheduled to speak at Moody Coliseum on the Southern Methodist University campus the following week. "This guy is great," the young man said. "You should get tickets and go."

So I did.

The lectures were scheduled to take place over a period of three evenings. I arrived for the first one eager to hear what this brilliant, experienced, thoughtful, eccentric man might say. To begin with, I found his unconventional physical appearance captivating. This diminutive man from the Alps looked a little more like Santa Claus than one of the great minds of our time. He was balding on top, had a long white beard, and was dressed in a white shirt with black knickers, white stockings, and black buckled shoes. He stood on the bare stage alone, behind a microphone supported by a slender stand, and spoke extemporaneously.

Dr. Schaeffer's lectures basically followed the material in his book, which I had not yet read, in which he theorized that there is a direct correlation between the decline of Christianity and the decline of Western Civilization.

First of all, I totally agreed that we seemed to be headed for hell in a hand basket. And what he was saying about Christianity made sense to me. In addition to believing that Christianity was a great crutch, I also believed that it was an excellent way to keep the general populace in check. As far as I was concerned, Karl Marx had hit it on the head when he called religion the opiate of the masses. And I thought that was a good thing. Clearly, if everyone followed the commandments laid out in the Bible, the troublemakers would calm down and the world would be a kinder, gentler, safer place to live.

That didn't mean me, of course. I might spend an occasional Sunday afternoon hanging out at Lee Park, but I wasn't out of control. And I was certainly no threat to society. I was managing just fine without any guidelines other than my personal moral code and the law of the land. I was part of the responsible group – the group that had no need for either the crutch or restrictions or the calming influence of Christianity.

The attentive audience in the coliseum included a large number of students who, judging from their questions at the end of each lecture, were primarily philosophy or theology majors at SMU. They delighted in challenging Dr. Schaeffer – trying to trip him up with their convoluted questions – all the while showing off their newly acquired brilliance in front of the large, captive audience. Far from being challenged, Dr. Schaeffer patiently fielded their questions with the ease of a softball coach knocking fly balls to his young outfielders.

I don't recall that there was anything religious about any of the three presentations. Dr. Schaeffer very sincerely and intelligently made his case that the societal structure that resulted from Western man's acceptance of Jesus Christ and His teachings was our civilization's only hope to halt the decline that would otherwise lead to our destruction.

Interwoven throughout the entire presentation was the fact that Jesus was more than just a great teacher who had all the answers. Dr. Schaeffer made it clear that he believed that Jesus was and is the only Son of God. I was a little surprised to hear that from a man with such an spectacular mind. But the rest of his message was exhilarating, and I was willing to overlook the "Jesus is God" part.

At the end of his lecture on the last day, Dr. Schaeffer did the first thing that could have been considered religious as opposed to purely intellectual. He said, "If you don't mind, I'd like to close with a word of prayer."

We all stood, and Dr. Schaeffer led us in a prayer – none of which I remember. At the end of the prayer, he thanked us for coming, turned to his right, and walked to the edge of the stage to go down the steps. I joined the other audience members who were headed toward the aisles to leave. I was delighted that the three evenings had been so intellectually stimulating, and had now turned my thoughts to choosing a restaurant where we could stop for dinner on the way home.

I happened to glance back just as Dr. Schaeffer reached the edge of the stage. I saw him suddenly turn and walk back to the microphone, and was surprised to hear him say, "Please wait."

Everyone stopped and turned back toward the small, soft-spoken man who was once again standing at the center of the huge, vacant stage.

"Please understand," he said, "that it is not vital that you believe this simply because it is necessary for the survival of our civilization – but because it's the truth."

I gasped and I almost fell. If the man had doused himself with gasoline and set himself ablaze, I wouldn't have been more stunned. I had the immediate physical sensation that something had exploded inside of me at the same time that someone had pushed me into a freezing lake.

I was no longer aware of anyone in Moody Coliseum except that one little man who, having spoken that single sentence, once again left the microphone and walked to the edge of the stage.

One minute before, I would have told you that Francis Schaeffer had, in fact, hit on something that made a great deal of sense to me when he discussed the positive impact that a belief in Jesus Christ and His teachings could have on those in our society who were responsible for the decline. I would also have said that, since I was not a problem to society, none of this had anything to do with me personally.

But now – *instantly and mysteriously* – my brain had totally reordered itself. I suddenly *knew* that Jesus Christ was the truth. And I intuitively recognized that I had probably been wrong about almost everything I thought I knew about how to live.

I looked around to see the reaction of the rest of the crowd to what I considered to be an absolutely astonishing statement by Dr. Schaeffer – a statement that caused a switch to be flipped inside my brain – that triggered a realization that I had just been given the key to the box that held all the answers. I looked from face to face for some sign that his statement had impacted someone else in the same way that it had impacted me. I wanted to shout, "Did you hear what he said?!?!?" But I quickly realized that, although they had heard, there was no epiphany for them. Everyone was now, once again, headed for the exits. I appeared to be the only one who had been struck blind on the road to Damascus.

I was so dumbfounded that I couldn't speak. I walked out of Moody Coliseum and rode home in bewildered silence, having completely forgotten about restaurants and eating.

When I walked into the house, all I could think about was a Bible I had been given 10 years earlier. Although I had studied the Bible as a child, I hadn't opened one in 15 years.

I searched my library and finally found that copy of the King James Bible. I opened the pages, which were still stuck together along their gilded edges, and began reading at Genesis 1:1. I read as far as the third chapter of Exodus, where Moses began trying to convince God that he was absolutely not the best person God could send to deliver the children of Israel out of Egypt.

Finally, Moses said to God, "…when I come unto the children of Israel, and shall say unto them, The God of your fathers hath sent me unto you; and they shall say to me, What is his name? What shall I say unto them? And God said unto Moses, I AM THAT I AM: and he said, Thus shalt thou say unto the children of Israel, I AM hath sent me unto you." (Exodus 3:13-14)

That verse was so powerful, and the emotion it evoked in me was so intense, that I had to close the book and put it down. I must surely have read that verse before. But now the old me had become new. Now, the new me perceived that verse as the most astonishing statement I had ever read in my life. I kept wondering what kind of being would call itself I AM. I AM THAT I AM!

I eventually read through the entire Bible, which resonated in my spirit with what I instinctively knew was the power of truth. I began to study the Word, and discovered a way of life that was entirely opposed to everything I thought I knew about how to live.

My spiritual journey began that day when the Holy Spirit sent Dr. Francis Schaeffer back to the microphone in Moody Coliseum on the SMU campus with a personal message for me. I don't believe that happened to me because I'm special. I believe it was a direct answer to the petitions of at least two powerful prayer warriors who, I later discovered, were praying for the Lord to draw me to Him.

What happened to me in that seminar did not happen in my head. It was neither logical nor intellectual. Nor was it initiated by me. I believe it was an invitation to me by God, at the request of the two dedicated believers who were praying for me. I had a choice in the matter, because we all have free will. I had a choice about whether or not to permit the Holy Spirit to reside in me. I could have said, "No." I could have closed the door and refused God's dramatic beckoning and continued to live my easy and satisfying life in just the same way that I had been living it for many years. In fact, I believe that many people say, "No."

But I said, "Yes."

Like most pilgrims who are progressing down their road of spiritual development, I have not been consistent in my pursuit of God's way. In fact, I have failed often and miserably in my attempt to be a doer of the Word and not a hearer only. But God has been consistent and faithful and merciful. Despite my failures, I have experienced His love and compassion as He has continued to patiently encourage me along my personal path toward a more intimate relationship with Him.

Because my path has been crooked and filled with mistakes and foolish decisions, my life is a superb example of how God continues to work with and through His imperfect children. One of the most dramatic ways that He has continued to manifest Himself in my life has been by allowing me to be a part of so many answered prayers.

My greatest hope is that, by reading about my experiences, you will be encouraged to embrace God and to implore Him to become an active partner in your life. I am very, very far from perfect. That's the point. We don't have to be. God is simply looking for people who are willing to strive every day, empowered by the help of the Holy Spirit, to present themselves as a living sacrifice – people with a commitment to cooperate with the Holy Spirit in the work that is necessary in order to produce clean hands and a pure heart, stretching toward God as they make themselves available to Him, striving to honor His commandment that we love Him and love one another.

I don't pretend to have all the answers. In fact, I'm not sure I have any. I can cite examples of answered prayer, but can't explain why. It always bothers me when people who survive a disaster proclaim that they're alive because God saved them while some poor praying mother beside them grieves for her dead child. Not only do I not have all the answers, I think we need to be wary of anyone who says they do.

But that shouldn't discourage us from praying. In fact, that should prod us on. The times that prayer "works" in a relatively short period of time should give us the encouragement to continue to pray. The times that it doesn't *appear* to "work" will be explained when we see Jesus face to face. We've all heard people say that all prayer is answered all the time; we just don't necessarily understand how. Maybe that's true.

What I do know is that your life and mine are filled with circumstances about which only we are aware – circumstances that will continue to go uncovered by the power of prayer if we don't move toward God and pray. Maybe you're the only one God can use in a particular situation. It is probable that if you refuse to make yourself available, there are people who will go unprotected and conditions that will continue to erode because God lacks an earthly partner.

I thank God that there were people who were willing to pray that the Lord would draw me to Him. It was God's answer to those prayers that rescued me from the world's pathetically superficial definition of success, and started me on the most glorious and most challenging journey of my life.

Chapter 2

The Wreck

Are not all angels ministering spirits sent to serve those who will inherit salvation? (Hebrews 1:14 NIV)

I had never prayed for the Lord's protection on a trip in my life before November 27, 1996. And I've never taken a trip without praying for safety since.

It was the Wednesday before Thanksgiving – the day some traffic cops call Black Wednesday because they can always count on a high number of traffic fatalities on that day. It had become our custom for my five-year-old daughter, Caroline, and me to go to Shreveport to visit with relatives who gathered from all over the country for a few days during Thanksgiving. My musician husband, Lynn, would stay in Baton Rouge to have dinner with his aging parents and spend some time working on his latest album. And that was our plan for this holiday.

Caroline and I were up early, eager to hit the road. She had gone to bed late the night before, and I knew she would be ready for a nap around noon.

We loaded the car and called Lynn's office to tell him we were leaving. I had to run a couple of errands before we left town, and noticed the heavy traffic as we made our way along the secondary roads. I knew that Interstate 10, which was always busy, would be more crowded than usual with travelers trying to get home for the holidays.

When we finished our last errand, I put Caroline in the back seat, belted her in, and got her settled for a nap with her little pink satin pillow and Winnie-the-Pooh blanket. I was actually looking forward to the four-hour drive. With Caroline sleeping most of the way, it would be a good time for me to meditate and enjoy some rare quiet time.

I got onto Interstate 10 via a ramp just east of the Mississippi River Bridge and moved my car into the center lane. We were not quite half way across the bridge when I felt a sudden and powerful urge to pray for our safety.

Now, when the Holy Spirit is leading me, there is no audible voice and the impulse doesn't originate in my head. It originates in my mid section, somewhere beneath my heart, and floats up to my unsuspecting brain. At that point, my mind, normally accustomed to being in control, is sometimes startled and always puzzled. This time was no different. But I acted without hesitation.

"Caroline," I called to see whether she was still awake.

"What, Mama?" she answered.

"We need to pray, Baby. Hold Mama's hand and let's pray."

I reached into the back seat and held her tiny hand as I implored the Lord to send angels before us to make our way safe, and to send angels to surround the car to protect us from harm and to prevent us from harming anyone else.

When I finished praying, I said, "Amen." I heard nothing from the back seat, so I prompted her. "Say amen, Baby."

"Amen, Mama," she said.

I looked at my clock. It was exactly 12:30.

Traffic had been a problem on the stretch of Interstate 10 from Baton Rouge to Lafayette for the previous year due to construction. And for some reason, the construction was never confined to one lane at a time. Instead, the work shifted back and forth, confusing drivers about which lane to use in order to keep moving.

At 12:45, just 15 minutes after Caroline and I had prayed, I was suddenly forced to stop in the left lane behind a long line of traffic. The Interstate at that point is lined on both sides with massive concrete guardrails that are designed to keep out-of-control vehicles from careening into the Atchafalaya Swamp.

As soon as my car came to a stop, I glanced into my rear-view mirror to see whether I could pull into the right lane. The instant I looked into the mirror, I saw an 18-wheeler, traveling at a high rate of speed, hit a small white car just four or five car lengths behind me. The driver of the white car apparently had not seen the truck, and had tried to switch to the right lane just as the truck was passing. The car glanced off to the left. The truck continued, now out of control, down the right lane of the Interstate.

I instinctively turned my steering wheel to the left, but there was no place for me to go. The cars were still stopped in front of me, and the guardrail on the left had me blocked. I knew that if that truck veered left, even a few feet, our car would be smashed between the immovable concrete guardrail and the speeding, out-of-control 18-wheeler. But there was nothing I could do.

As I sat, breathlessly gripping the steering wheel, with my eyes frozen on the rear-view mirror, the 18-wheeler suddenly jerked to the right. I was stunned to see the right side tires jump over the guardrail, and the truck, with the left tires on the road and the right tires riding the top of the guardrail, continue toward us. As the truck proceeded down the Interstate, tilted at this precarious angle, the horrible sound of the truck's underbelly grinding against the concrete was deafening.

The truck had been traveling at such a high rate of speed that even this didn't stop the forward thrust. It continued toward us, leaning to the left, for what seemed like an impossibly long time. I didn't pray.

I didn't even breathe. I just stared, unblinkingly, at the enormous, threatening mass of steel as it came closer and closer and closer.

As I watched in horror, the truck finally began to slow. It lost its momentum just as the front bumper of the truck was even with the back bumper of my car.

I had not started breathing again before I turned to the back seat to check on Caroline. I knew the sound would have frightened her. I was amazed to see her sleeping peacefully, with that enormous truck leaning so close to her that if the sun had been shining from the north, it would have cast a shadow on her face.

I jumped out of my car and ran to the cab of the truck. Just as I got there, the driver opened the door. Because the truck was still resting at an angle, the driver fell onto the Interstate. I helped him steady himself. I looked at him closely and saw that, although dazed, he wasn't hurt. He asked me if he had hit the car, but I was to traumatized to speak. I looked to my right and saw a man leaning into the small white car that had been hit, caring for the people in that vehicle. I looked to my left and saw two women running toward us to try to help.

Then I smelled diesel fuel.

Since the accident happened, I have learned that diesel fuel is not nearly as flammable as gasoline. But I didn't know that at the time. All I could think of at that point was that I had a child in the back seat of my car and flammable liquid was spilling around and under that car.

By this time, vehicles were backed up on the Interstate behind us as far as I could see. I knew that those who were involved in the accident, none of whom appeared to be hurt, would be helped by all the people who by now were running toward us. The truck driver began trying to stuff rags and towels into the openings in the guardrail, in an apparent attempt to prevent the diesel fuel from running into the swampy water below. I never spoke a single word to anyone. I just stumbled back to my car and drove away.

I was so grateful that Caroline was still sleeping. I felt mentally and physically numb, and I knew I was in no condition to explain any of this to her. My brain simply wasn't able to process anything that had happened.

I was in a stupor for the rest of the day. I couldn't escape the image of the out-of-control 18-wheeler bearing down on us. When I arrived in Shreveport, I told my parents about the accident, but I realize now that I was in shock and wasn't able to fully convey the seriousness of what had happened. No matter what I was doing, even while I was talking to someone, I continued to see the giant truck coming toward me. It seemed to me that I was viewing everything through a transparency of the approaching 18-wheeler.

I finally got to sleep that night. But when I woke up the next morning, the image of the truck, as it was reflected in the mirror, was still before my eyes. I helped Mother with Thanksgiving dinner and made conversation, but I was still dazed, still seeing everything through the transparent image of the truck.

Finally, dinner was ready and we began to put the food on the table. Mother had prepared a large casserole dish full of sweet potatoes, and the dish had been sitting on the stove, cooling. She picked up the casserole dish, and turned to take it to the table. Then, for no apparent reason, she suddenly dropped the dish. The sound of the glass dish smashing on the hard kitchen floor was as loud as a shotgun blast. Instantly, the image of the truck evaporated from my mind's eye, and it never returned. The fog that had surrounded me immediately lifted, and I felt like I was back to normal.

We had a wonderful Thanksgiving dinner followed by a couple of delightful days of visiting with my family. It wasn't until the trip home that I had enough quiet time to really think about what had happened.

As I drove south toward Baton Rouge, reflecting on our near disaster of a few days earlier, I was reminded of something a Bible study leader once concluded in one of her lectures. She said, "Friends, God didn't just put us here and then go off and leave us to gut it out on our own."

I so strongly believe that's true. I believe with all of my heart that He wants to help us. But the system He has set up doesn't permit Him to act unilaterally – to pull our strings like a puppeteer manipulating little wooden dolls. It appears that God needs the cooperation – perhaps at times even the permission – of a human being in order to become actively involved in our lives.

I still sometimes think of how helpless I felt the day that truck came barreling toward us from behind. But now, the fear has been replaced with gratitude that the Holy Spirit warned me that I would need the assistance of the angels. And that's the memory that comes to my mind every Thanksgiving when Caroline and I pray for safe travel as we head home for the holidays.

Chapter 3

My Best Friend Margaret

*There are "friends" who pretend to be friends, but there is a friend who
sticks closer than a brother (Proverbs 18:24 TLB)*

I always had a group of girlfriends when I was growing up, but
I never had a best friend. When I was in my early teens, there
was a girl my age who lived down the street. Her name was Jan. I
frequently spent time at Jan's house, but I think it was more about
ease and convenience than any special attraction. Because she lived
so close, I didn't have to ask my mother to take me anywhere. All I

had to do was climb out my bedroom window (because the distance from my window to her house was shorter than from my front door) and walk down to the end of the block. Jan's mother usually had a pot of beans and a pan of cornbread on the stove, and I would sometimes partake of their bounty before we retreated to Jan's room – away from her pesky little brother and sister. My most vivid memory is of the two of us closed up in her bedroom, spraying an entire can of hairspray on our hair so we could be sure it would not move if we unexpectedly had to go outside and inadvertently got caught in a breeze. It's a miracle we didn't asphyxiate ourselves.

I had a lot of male friends in high school. I found it easier to relate to guys. They seemed to be more honest and straightforward and – well – simpler in their approach to life. I liked the fact that they weren't petty or gossipy.

As I got older, I just found men more interesting. My mind seemed to work in a way that our society has traditionally considered to be typically male. I tended to be more cerebral than emotional – more analytical than intuitive. I was confident and independent, had an edge of cynicism, and could be alarmingly blunt. When I was in my late 20s and going to lots of parties, I would usually end up hanging out with the guys, discussing politics and government and world affairs and watching football while the women were in another room discussing whatever it is that women discuss.

I distinctly remember one such time when I was sitting in someone's living room with the men, thoroughly enjoying the conversation about the most troublesome world crisis of the moment, when I happened to look to my left and see the women gathered around a baby while its mother changed its diaper. The women were involved in a lengthy discussion about the advantages of one particular brand of diaper over another, and seemed to be enjoying themselves. I remember being genuinely puzzled at how in the name of the Lord they could possibly find the subject of diapers so interesting that they could discuss it for more than 10 seconds.

I worked with men, and remember when one of them complimented me by saying, "Sandy looks like a woman, thinks like a man, and works like a horse." In this politically correct age, that might get him slapped with a sexual harassment suit. But I was flattered.

I suppose part of my inclination was influenced by my identification with my father, with whom I had been holding political discussions since I was 12 years old. But some of it was simply attributable to my inherent mental and emotional makeup. Regardless of the reason, the end result was a personality that was not particularly well suited to being best friends with a female who liked to do things like have manicures and go shopping and talk a lot.

So, I was in my mid-30s, contentedly living my life without a best friend, when the adult education minister at my church, Courtney, arrived at my house accompanied by two other women. They were there because Courtney had told us that we all four believed the same thing about prayer – namely that it is powerful – and she wanted us to meet one another and form a prayer group. One of those two women was Margaret.

Margaret grew up in Levelland, Texas – just 30 miles west of Lubbock. Her parents, as is so often the case, were more wrapped up in their own personal dysfunction than in rearing their children. So, except for her grandmother, Margaret was pretty much on her own to figure out whatever needed to be figured out. She and her sister, Rose, were wonderful singers. When they were in their mid-teens – displaying the courage and zest for adventure that will surprise you only if you've never known anyone from West Texas – they ran away from home. Destination: Chicago. Mission: Sing background for Dale Hawkins. They were cutting an album as a follow up to Hawkins' hit single "Suzie Q," and they would be working with the legendary Leonard Chess at Chess Records.

That was the official beginning of Margaret's career. By the time I met her at my front door, she had spent most of her life in the music business. She had most recently worked as a singer and songwriter in Nashville, and had returned to Shreveport when she married her childhood sweetheart, Alton. And she was probably the antithesis of what I would have looked for if someone had forced me to go out and find a best friend.

Margaret is a short, fluffy-haired blonde, and I immediately recognized her to be a vivacious, warm woman who is eager to make everyone feel welcome and comfortable and included. She's sort of a female Andy Hardy, likely to jump up at any moment and encourage everyone to work together to decorate the barn and build a stage and put on a show. I came to also know her as an extremely intuitive woman who ran a little low on self-confidence and had no real passion for world affairs or sports.

She recalls that first meeting at my house. I served Perrier and fruit and bran muffins, and Margaret mentioned that she should have brought some donuts. My reply, according to Margaret, was, "I don't do donuts." I must admit that sounds like me.

So I ask you: If you were a matchmaker of best friends, would you have put us together? I didn't think so. Neither would I. Isn't it wonderful that God is so much smarter than either of us. As it turns out, He was involved in this meeting from the beginning.

Margaret, as I later learned, had moved to Shreveport knowing very few people. She had developed lots of acquaintances and casual friends. But she wanted a really good friend. So she began to pray for God to send her a best friend.

Margaret would have welcomed my friendship with open arms. That's just the way she is. However, I'm sure you will not be surprised to hear that I would probably never have been interested in getting to know Margaret. I just wasn't particularly drawn to fluffy, blonde country singer/songwriters who were (I forgot to mention this one) *always* late for *everything*. But, as I got to know her heart through spending hours in a prayer group with her, our friendship grew. And I eventually learned that she is extremely smart, enormously creative, fiercely loyal, and one of the most sincerely and deeply spiritual people I've ever known. Because her outward appearance and demeanor contradict the complexity of what's inside, a mutual friend once described Margaret as the most consistently underrated person she's ever known.

I've learned a number of lessons from my friendship with Margaret. The first is obvious. We make such huge mistakes when we judge people by their exterior that I think we really should just all give up on that system entirely. But even more lessons have been launched from this friendship that now spans 20-something years.

As it turns out, we each ended up where you might have expected the other to be. I, the cerebral one who didn't relate to women *at all* – the one who graduated from college and derived much of my personal worth from my career and had not ever thought children were in my future – ended up as a stay-at-home mom dealing with women all the time as a school volunteer, scout leader, Bible study leader, and a host of other positions that produce no income and require a great deal more finesse than intellect. Margaret, the girlie one who just loved everybody and liked to sing and write songs and would have loved to have a baby, ended up heading a project that is well on its way to becoming something as big as Disney World.

Why, we might ask, would that be so? Well – as anyone who knows me will not be surprised to hear, I have a theory.

We all know that God uses our strengths and talents. But I believe that is only part of the story. I believe that the experiences we have in life, once we give ourselves to God, are largely engineered to strengthen our withered side. The idea is to force us into the position of having to reshape ourselves into a whole, balanced person whom God can use in a more significant way than if we are overdeveloped in some areas and underdeveloped in others.

If I had ended up as chairman of Margaret's project, that would have reinforced my more assertive characteristics that are traditionally considered more masculine. If Margaret had ended up as a mother, working as a school volunteer, it would have reinforced her traditionally female characteristics. Instead, I've been put in a position where I've had to become more flexible, soften my style, and begin to actually care (at least a *little*) about whether people like me – primarily because of the impact it ultimately has on my daughter. Margaret, on the other hand, has been forced to toughen up, to think things through rather than act instinctively, to develop a more businesslike manner, and to understand that the only way you accomplish anything significant in the business world is to stop caring whether everyone likes you.

Life has not been as easy as it would have been if God had placed us according to our strengths and talents. We've both had to stretch in order to meet the obligations and the demands that are made on us as we attempt to bloom where God has planted us. But we're better people because we've had to stretch.

In addition to making us better people, our friendship has also provided us with companionship along the rough road of life in a most miraculous way. Although we operate in very different worlds – I in the land of domesticity and Margaret in the arena of business and high finance – our struggles have paralleled in a way that continues to astonish both of us. We talk often, and are frequently amazed that we're wrestling with the same problem at the same time, just on a different level. Because of that, we are able to recognize that what we're going through is not just random. We can see that God has a grand plan – that there is a purpose for the struggles we're experiencing – and that He arranged this special friendship so that we could walk this walk together and encourage one another. Our parallel experiences reinforce the fact that no matter how bleak things look sometimes, we're in God's school, and He's guiding our education in a way that draws us closer to becoming the kind of people He wants us to be.

When I look back over all these years, I find it amusing that I didn't even think I needed a best friend. Fortunately, Margaret had the good sense to pray for one. The benefits I have received from our relationship are immeasurable, and for that I will be grateful to her for eternity.

Chapter 4

Kathy's Ride to the Store

And it shall come to pass, that before they call, I will answer; and while
they are yet speaking, I will hear. (Isaiah 65:24)

Most families with multiple siblings have one member who
stands out as just a little more colorful than the others. In my
family of origin, although we've all had our moments, the titleholder
for most colorful of the four sisters would have to be Kathy.

Kathy spent most of the '70s and '80s and '90s in denial that the
'60s had ended. She preferred the music, the clothing, and the life-

style represented by the golden era of the hippie. I would sometimes say to her, "Kathy, the '60s are over!" She would always reply, with a blissful smile on her face, "I know. But I _loved_ the '60s."

The drug world and motorcycle gangs and living on the dark side characterized certain segments of Kathy's life. Despite periodic attempts at change, she just seemed more comfortable with a lifestyle that included black leather and tattoos and walking on the wild side.

My sister's choice of men was about as predictable as her other behaviors. She leaned toward short men with long hair who had very little respect for women. The version at the moment, Steve, was no different.

The two of them were currently living in the middle of nowhere in rural Mississippi in Steve's recently deceased grandmother's house. Kathy knew no one in the area, had no income of her own, and had no access to transportation when Steve was gone on his Harley.

It didn't take hours of reflection to figure out that this girl needed help on a number of levels. But I knew I couldn't fix her life. I didn't think anyone could help her at that particular time. When we talked on the phone, I just didn't hear in her voice any of the strength and resolve necessary for change.

So my three prayer partners, Courtney and Margaret and Barbara, joined in agreement with me as we began to storm the gates of heaven on Kathy's behalf. We prayed unceasingly. We knew that we didn't have any answers or any power to help her, but we knew that God had the answers. We trusted Him to honor our prayers and help Kathy.

I will be eternally grateful that I had prayer partners, powerful women of God, who did not for one moment judge my sister or her life style. They understood that we have to meet people where they are, even when they don't seem to be as far along on their personal path with God as we think they should be. We don't ever know what God has in mind. Some people seem to stall for a while, then suddenly shoot ahead of those who have called themselves children of God all their lives. The judgment and the timing are better left to God. Our job is to love people and pray for them.

Several weeks after we began to pray for Kathy, she called me, sounding absolutely mystified, to tell me about something that had happened to her the day before. She said that she and Steve had fought, and he had left on his motorcycle – their only mode of transportation. Did I mention that they lived in the middle of nowhere? Steve had been gone for several days, and had not contacted Kathy. It had reached the point that she had very little food in the kitchen, and was down to her last of everything in the bathroom.

"I didn't know what to do," she said. "I didn't know anyone to call for help. Well, yesterday morning, I went into the bathroom and took a shower and washed my hair with the last of the shampoo. Then I dried my hair and got dressed. When I finished, I walked out the back door of the house and sat down on the steps.

"And then," she said, "for some reason, I just said out loud, 'Jesus, I need a ride to the store.'"

Kathy said that at the precise moment that those words left her lips, a blue Ford LTD pulled off the main highway in front of the farmhouse and into her driveway. The car stopped near the steps where Kathy was sitting and a man got out. As the man walked toward her, Kathy recognized him as someone she had met once before. He was the owner of the tree trimming company where Steve worked.

The man spoke to her and reminded her that Steve worked for him. Then he said, "I am so sorry to have to ask you for your help. But I really need to get back to work. My problem is that my wife doesn't know how to drive and she really needs to go to the store. Do you mind taking my car and driving her to the store?"

Kathy said she sat, stunned, staring at this unlikely messenger from God – a messenger who had pulled into the driveway at the exact moment that her plea to Jesus had left her mouth. That meant that he was driving toward her house while she was still in the shower, before she had walked outside to sit on the steps, before she had even thought about forming her little one-sentence prayer to Jesus.

Before she called out for help, God had answered.

The God who parted the Red Sea and gave Joshua victory at the battle of Jericho cared enough to reach down, in answer to our prayers and hers, and help my little sister – despite the fact that she was not exactly living a life that would thrill Him. He gave His time and attention to arranging for her to have a ride to the store in some little backwoods Mississippi town so she could buy kitchen and bathroom essentials – before she even asked. Before she called, He answered.

I would like to report that this incident so impressed Kathy that she immediately turned her life over to God and served Him faithfully from that moment forward. Unfortunately, her progress has been more like mine. If charted, it would probably resemble the performance of some of the more erratic stocks in recent Wall Street memory.

I am pleased to report, however, that she now lives with her cat (the bravest and most beautiful cat I've ever known) and her dog (the most beautiful and most rambunctious dog I've ever known) in her own adorable little house with crosses hanging on the wall. She has a job that she truly enjoys, and experience seems to have taught her some lessons about how to avoid complicating her life. And when she finds herself in a difficult spot of any kind, she always makes sure that I get word to pray for her.

If you've hesitated to pray for your more colorful friends and relatives because you think that's just too much of a stretch for God, reconsider. Like the father of the prodigal son, our Father wants us all to come back to Him. And He's willing to perform miracles in order to draw us closer to home.

Chapter 5

Daddy Doesn't Want a Dog

Rest in the Lord, and wait patiently for him.... (Psalms 37:7)

My daughter came into this world with an intense love for animals. All animals. By the time she was three years old, she was engaging us in serious conversations about what she should get first – a cat or a dog or a horse.

We live downtown, so a horse seemed seriously unwise – not to mention illegal. I don't mind cats, but I must confess to being a lover of dogs. So, since I knew I would end up taking care of the pet, I decided we should start with what I would most like to spend my time hanging out with – and that would be a dog. I reasoned, rightly or wrongly, that it should be a small dog for our small girl.

With my mind made up about the kind of animal we needed to start with, I decided to mention it to Lynn when he got home that night. I casually explained my logic in a typical FYI tone of voice, expecting that he might only be half listening because he would be so uninterested. Imagine my surprise when, at the end of my announcement, he said, "No."

No?

At first I thought he might have misunderstood what I said. I mean, it was just a dog. And don't all kids have a dog? He had a dog when he was growing up. I had a dog when I was growing up. It had never occurred to me that he would care one way or the other – just so long as he didn't have to take care of the little critter.

But I looked at his face, and his expression told me that he was, in fact, actually listening to me and that his "no" had been spoken consciously and purposefully.

He came up with an impressive list of excuses. He didn't want to deal with vet bills, he didn't want an animal in the house, he didn't like small dogs, he was afraid Caroline would get bitten, and on and on and on.

I couldn't believe what I was hearing. It had never even entered my mind that he might not go along with us, especially because Caroline was pretty passionate about this whole deal. Besides, I wasn't asking his permission! I was informing him, for Pete's sake!

Now, I have never been described as a shrinking violet. I am strong-willed, independent, confident in my ability to accurately analyze situations, and comfortable making my own decisions. I'll have to admit that it crossed my mind to go get a dog for my begging child and deal with the consequences when the time came. But it doesn't take a Bible scholar to know that God would not be thrilled with me thumbing my nose at my husband. And one of the top priorities in my life is making God happy.

So I waited. And Caroline kept begging.

I talked to people about dogs and dreamed about dogs and read about dogs. I knew exactly what I wanted her to have. My cousin, Debbie, had a Pekipoo (half Pekinese and half Poodle) that I thought was adorable. Debbie's was brown, but I wanted Caroline's Pekipoo to be white. I had never seen a white Pekipoo, mind you, but I was convinced that's what Caroline needed.

I had it all figured out, you see. But Lynn was not budging. And experience had taught me that it was pointless to try to nag him into acquiescence.

One day in the midst of all of this, I took Caroline to a near-by lake to feed the ducks. There was a young couple there with a beautiful little fluffy white puppy that completely ignored its owners and romped with Caroline for almost an hour. Caroline laughed so much as she played with that puppy that she would almost lose her breath.

I will admit that if I had known where to go to get a puppy like that one, I might have been tempted to give up on my determination to honor God by honoring Lynn's wishes. It was so hard to watch her enjoy something as much as she enjoyed that puppy and not get one for her.

Isn't that always the way it happens? When we're striving to do what we know God wants us to do, circumstances seem to conspire to ramp up the pressure to go the other way. It's the modern day equivalent of the serpent whispering in our ear. "Go on," he says. "Eat the apple. You won't really die, you silly girl."

I'm a little ashamed to admit that praying about this had not entered my mind before. But that day, I realized that I needed to pray for a puppy – and for God's grace to wait until one arrived. I thought that if someone would suddenly show up at my door with a puppy, Lynn would know it was from God and wouldn't have the heart to refuse. Then we would have what we wanted without blatantly disregarding his wishes.

So I prayed that God would send a puppy.

And I prayed and prayed.

I expected an angel to float to my front door, hand Lynn a puppy, and say, "God wants your daughter to have this, you silly man." As usual, God didn't do this the way I expected.

One Saturday morning, Lynn and I were sitting on the deck reading the paper while Caroline played in the back yard. We had not discussed dogs for several weeks. I was determined to pray and keep my mouth shut.

Suddenly, with absolutely no previous indication that he was having second thoughts about the issue of the dog, Lynn said, "They're having pet adoption day today. Why don't y'all go check it out?"

What?!?!? I almost fell out of my chair. What?!?!? I managed to maintain my composure and calmly said, "OK," as though I weren't the least bit surprised. I was, in fact, shocked! I was thrilled! My prayers had been answered!

Caroline and I raced each other to the car and headed for the address given in the paper. We arrived in front of a small metal building where we saw a parking lot full of cars and people going in and out with big dogs on leashes and kittens in carriers. We walked into the building just as a man was registering three black puppies to be adopted. Caroline picked up one of the puppies, her eyes began to shine, and she clutched that puppy with all the strength that a four-year-old girl could muster.

I was delighted that she had found a puppy she liked. It wasn't exactly the white Pekipoo I had in mind, but I figured God was in charge here and I would go along with whatever He thought was best. I filled out the adoption papers and waited while the volunteers screened our application.

As one of the volunteers approached us, I could tell something was wrong. She was polite and apologetic when she said, "Mrs. Ourso, we try to be very careful about our placements. We're concerned about the fact that you don't have a fenced yard. I won't tell you that you can't have this puppy," she continued. "But he's part lab and part beagle. If he catches a scent, he'll be gone and you'll never see him again."

Caroline, understanding enough of what was being said to know there was a problem, was staring at me with terror in her eyes. There were no other puppies to consider. I was filled with dread at the thought of prying this one out of her arms. But I was filled with even more dread at the thought of her getting attached to a dog that would run away and never be seen again.

"Honey, we can't take this puppy because he needs a fenced yard," I said.

I've never seen anyone cry like that. The tears weren't even touching her cheeks. They were just shooting out of her eyes.

She cried all the way home. I almost went back for the puppy twice. The only thing that stopped me was the thought of how much worse it would be if she got attached to the dog and then it ran away. She wasn't old enough to understand the practicality of the decision I had just made, and nothing I said could comfort her. All she understood was that one moment she had a puppy and the next moment she didn't. And my reassurances that we would find another dog were not working. She was devastated.

For that matter, so was I. I thought this whole thing had been God's idea, that I was following His lead. I had done everything the way I thought He wanted me to. I had waited and kept my mouth shut and prayed and trusted Him. But it didn't seem to be working out very well.

I don't know whether this is a pattern in other people's lives, but it is in mine. Often, I'll think I've heard from God and proceed – only to have the whole thing appear to be on the right track for a period of time, but then quickly fall apart or seem to go wrong. I sometimes wonder if that's not God giving us a chance to decide which way we'll go – whether we'll choose to curse Him and give up, or elect to persist with a more mature level of faith in order to see things through to the blessing.

By the time Caroline and I got home, she had used up all of her tears. I called our little neighbor, Abbie, to come over and play with Caroline in order to get her mind off the dog. As they began to play, I opened the paper to the classified section. The first thing I saw was an advertisement for Pekipoo puppies for sale.

By this time, it was noon. I figured they were probably all sold by now. But I decided to call anyway.

"We only have two left," said the man who answered, "and I have someone who said they would be over shortly to pick up one."

I didn't even ask what color they were. I just said, "I'm on my way for the other one."

I hung up the phone, told Lynn about the conversation, and we agreed that the girls should stay at home with him and we wouldn't tell them where I was going. I couldn't go through seeing Caroline disappointed again if this didn't work out.

The puppies were in Walker, a town about 45 minutes from Baton Rouge. As I headed east, the storm that had been threatening all day produced a black sky that served up a pretty impressive South Louisiana downpour. It took me longer than I'd expected to make the trip. I was concerned that the breeder might let the last puppy go with someone else if I didn't get there in what he considered to be a reasonable time. I passed the house once. I wasn't sure why, but I didn't think it looked like a home. When I circled back, I saw the house numbers and realized that I was in the right place. I parked my car and went to the door.

When the man answered the door, I told him that I was held up by the rain and had passed the house once. "People pass us up all the time," he said. "This used to be a church. My wife and I bought it and converted it into a house.

"Come on around to the side," he said. "The people who called haven't gotten here yet. Probably because of this weather."

I met him at the side entrance of the house, and he led me into a room where I saw the mother. She was a beautiful, silky white Pekinese who was still nursing the runt of the litter. The owner took me to a child's play pen in the center of the room, and I looked down on two of the most adorable little white Pekipoo puppies I could ever have hoped to see.

The puppies were six weeks old. I later calculated that they were conceived at about the time I started praying for a puppy.

I picked up the little male – thinking Lynn might like the dog better if it was a male – and wrapped him in towels to protect him from the rain. I stopped for puppy food and then drove home, thrilled with the thought of Caroline's reaction when she got her first glimpse of the puppy.

When I walked into the house, Caroline and Abbie were sitting at the breakfast bar eating peanut butter and jelly sandwiches. I just walked over and laid the blue towel in front of them. The girls looked at one another in disbelief when the towel began to move. As soon as the puppy's nose made its way out of the towel, Caroline cried, "It's a puppy!"

What a day. And what a dog. He and Caroline romp and wrestle and play for hours, and Caroline laughs until she loses her breath.

One of the most delightful surprises that came out of all of this is the relationship between Lynn and the dog. Caroline and I named the dog Sugar, but Lynn and his daddy were outraged at such an inappropriate name for a male. They changed his name to King. King's full-grown weight is only six pounds, but he thinks he's a Doberman. He's a high-spirited, energetic guard dog that likes to play rough and is protective of Caroline. And he adores Lynn. Several months after we got him, Lynn told me that the dog was the best idea I ever had.

I've often thought how differently things would have evolved if I had taken matters into my own hands and gone against Lynn's will instead of praying and waiting. Someone once said that every single "no" is just a way to get us to God's greater "yes." However, in order to reach that greater "yes," we can't fall down on the floor kicking and screaming when we get the "no." We have to keep moving forward in faith, confident that God knows a lot of stuff we don't know.

I could have fallen down kicking and screaming when Lynn said "no" to the dog. Instead, I kept my attitude right (Thank you, Jesus!) and moved forward by praying and waiting for God to handle the situation in His perfect time. In doing so, I got everything I wanted plus the bonus of peace and tranquility in my home.

Actually, there is one more interesting part to the story. When King was five years old, we decided it was time to get a second dog. I called the breeder from whom I bought King. His wife answered, and I told her we would be interested in buying another white Pekipoo when they had their next litter. "Oh, we won't have any," she said. "I'm not even sure why we did it that time. We don't like to cross breed because the results are so unpredictable. That's the only time we ever did that."

What a precious God we serve.

Chapter 6

The Holy Spirit and the Olympic Bomb

The effectual, fervent prayer of a righteous man availeth much.
(James 5:16)

For as by one man's disobedience many were made sinners, so by the obedience of one shall many be made righteous. (Romans 5:19)

"I am so tired," said Margaret at the end of one of our frequent long-distance conversations. "But I'm really looking forward to this, and I know the guys in the band are, too."

I knew she must be exhausted. She had just performed at the Smithsonian for two weeks and then had to go to Georgia to play at a private party only two days after returning to Louisiana from Washington. Now, after only a few days rest, she and her band were headed to Atlanta where they would perform nightly at the Olympics for a week.

Margaret and I had been best friends for many years. We spoke almost every day and we never stopped praying together, even though most of those prayers had been over long-distance phone lines since I had moved to the opposite end of the state. When we hung up on this particular day, I didn't expect that we would talk again until she returned from Atlanta.

A few days later, on Friday evening, July 26, 1996, I ate dinner at home with Lynn and Caroline. When we finished, I cleared the table while they went into the den to do two of their favorite things – play music and dance.

I had finished the dishes and was walking down the hall toward the back of the house when I suddenly felt an urgent need to pray for Margaret's safety. As much as she and her husband traveled, I had never even thought about praying for their safety before. But it was absolutely clear to me at that moment that I need to pray immediately.

I turned into the bathroom, closed the door to shut out the music coming from the den, and knelt beside the bathtub to pray. As I began to pray, I felt a burdened that was so oppressive that I began to cry. I tearfully petitioned God to watch over Margaret and her husband, Alton, and to keep them out of harm's way.

I continued to cry and pray for some period of time before I gradually began to feel the burden lift. I prayed until the tears stopped and I felt peace in my spirit that I had done what I was supposed to do. Then I thanked God for protecting them, got up, dried my eyes, and went back to my chores.

But I felt puzzled as I went through my routine that night and on to bed. I knew Margaret was probably either on her way to the Olympic grounds or was already on stage performing. I decided to wait until the next morning to call her to tell her what had happened.

The next morning I woke up later than usual. Our little neighbor, Abbie, came over to ask if Caroline could go to her house to play. We woke Caroline, got her dressed, and I stood on the back deck for a while as I watched them walk through my yard toward Abbie's house.

When they were out of sight,   I turned to go back into the house to get dressed. As I walked through the door, I heard the answering machine click. When I pressed the "play" button to find out what call I had just missed, I heard Margaret's voice.

"It's me, checking in from Atlanta," she said. "I don't know whether y'all heard about the bomb or not. We performed last night at 9:00 on a stage about half a block from where the bomb went off. We left the park about 11:00, and all of our group got out OK. We were scheduled to perform today on a stage near where the bomb went off, but all of the events have been cancelled for today."

I turned to Lynn, who had now entered the room, and stared at him, speechless. "Oh, I forgot to tell you," he said. "A bomb exploded at the Olympics last night, and a bunch of people were hurt."

I was overwhelmed with emotion. I immediately understood what had happened, and it was later confirmed by Margaret.

She later told me that after the band performed, there had been some discussion about remaining on the Olympic grounds. They were all hungry, and wanted to get something to eat. However, after some debate, they finally decided they were just too tired. So they all went back to the hotel. If they had stayed to eat, they would probably have still been in the vicinity of the bomb when it exploded.

I don't claim to have all the answers about how God's system works. In fact, I don't think I even have all the questions. But there must be a reason that the Holy Spirit prompted me to pray. It may be that God needed me to pray in order to protect Margaret and Alton. And if that is true, it is reckless for us to go blithely about our lives, unprotected by a covering of prayer for ourselves and our loved ones, simply leaving it all to chance.

I know that some people believe that it is presumptuous of us to think that God needs us for anything. But it seems to me that when God gave man authority over the earth, He limited His own right to interfere in the earth. Most Biblical accounts of God's dealings with mankind and the earth involve the cooperation of a person.

In deference to those who have prayed for a loved one to be healed and then watched them die, I repeat that I don't have all the answers. If we could put the pope and Billy Graham together in one room and hammer them with questions, we still wouldn't be able to come up with all the answers. What I do know is that in Luke 18:1, Jesus told his disciples that they should always pray and not give up. I don't think that God, through His Word, is encouraging us to participate in an exercise in futility.

Prayer changes things. That doesn't mean that God is a gumball machine. I'm pretty sure that it's more complicated than that. But some really amazing things have happened in my life, and even more amazing things in the lives of countless other people, as a result of prayer. It behooves us all to educate ourselves in the practice of prayer – to aggressively study what God's Word has to say about how we need to pray – all the while understanding that we won't know everything about how the system works until we get to glory and ask Jesus.

You may not see an answer to every prayer. They don't all get answered over night. Even when they do, we don't necessarily recognize it as an answer because it's so often not what we had in mind. But the percentage of prayers that you recognize as answered will be high enough for you to know that it's a great deal more than just luck.

Chapter 7

Lord, I Can't Stand Ben

*But the Lord said unto Samuel, Look not on his countenance, or on the
height of his stature; because I have refused him: for the Lord seeth not
as a man seeth; for man looketh on the outward appearance,
but the Lord looketh on the heart. (I Samuel 16:7)*

His name was Ben, and I couldn't stand to be around him.
I knew that was the wrong way to feel. I knew God was not
happy with me. But I just couldn't seem to stop. I cringed when I
saw him coming. The problem was that, since Ben and I belonged

to the same church, and were both very active members, I saw him coming often. Too often!

Ben pretty much represented a majority of the things I found unattractive in a man. He was short and fat, had little formal education, and wore cheap polyester suits and fake leather cowboy boots. And, worst of all, he was never prepared for teaching his Sunday School class because he thought he knew enough to "wing it." On top of all that, I couldn't find anything to offset the negative. I mean – he wasn't naturally funny or naturally brilliant or…well, you get the idea.

But every time I turned around, there was Ben!

One day I decided that I needed to somehow deal with the fact that God couldn't be thrilled with my attitude about Ben. Out of desperation, because no amount of self-discipline seemed adequate to force an attitude change, I decided to start praying for him.

I didn't know enough about Ben's life to know of any specific area where he might need help, so I just started praying that the Lord would shower Ben with His blessings. I had met Ben's wife and two children, so I also prayed for them. I prayed for the four of them every day as though they were four of my best friends.

And the most amazing thing began to happen.

After only one week of prayer for Ben, I honestly, and with absolutely no effort on my part, began to see him and his situation differently. I began to realize that I was not the only one who recognized that Ben was very different from the comfortable, well-heeled, well-educated crowd that attended our church. Ben recognized it, too. Although he made a valiant effort, an occasional fleeting look of bewilderment would reveal his awareness that he wasn't quite in sync with the rest of us.

I had often wondered why he joined our church in the first place. There were so many churches of the same denomination in our community – churches that had congregations with which Ben would have been better able to relate. What I learned from a mutual acquaintance was that Ben had been in a meeting in another city with our pastor, had felt strongly drawn to the man, and had joined the church because of that sense of spiritual connection. Since I, too, held our pastor in very high regard, that impressed me.

As I continued to pray for Ben, more snippets of information about him began to mysteriously make their way to my ears. I began to put the pieces of the puzzle together, and a new picture of Ben seemed to emerge. I soon recognized that he was a good husband and loving father. He was a sincere, devoted Christian man who had joined our church because of his respect for our pastor, and probably found himself committed before he realized that he didn't fit in. But he didn't leave once he realized the difference. Instead, he decided to stay and do the best he could, despite his very demanding work situation, to become an active member of the congregation.

I began to have respect for the man's faithfulness despite his lack of sufficient time to prepare, his willingness to participate in all activities despite the fact that he didn't look or dress like the rest of us, his obvious devotion to his family, and his commitment to rearing his children in a Godly home. And ultimately, through no effort of my own, I actually reached the point that I was genuinely happy to see Ben walking toward me down the church corridor.

I thank God for using Ben to put me in a place that was so uncomfortable for me. Because I knew it didn't please God, I was forced to ask for the help of the Holy Spirit in finding my way to an attitude that *would* be pleasing to God. And that way, of course, is always the way of love.

I was reminded of all of this recently when I watched a popular comedian who hosts a highly rated news program on cable TV. He concluded a segment in which he was making fun of the hosts of an international Christian TV network by saying, "If God has a message for me, He's not going to send it through some woman with *big, pink hair!*"

A few days later, I was relating that incident to my best friend, Margaret. I loved her response. "Oh yes He will," she said. "That's part of the test."

That whole outward appearance thing was part of the test that tripped up the Jews after Jesus began his ministry. They were looking for a messiah, but Jesus wasn't at all what they had envisioned. He was, of all things, a carpenter from Nazareth. He couldn't have been any more wrong, as far as they were concerned, if he'd shown up with big pink hair.

I am pleased to report that, with the help of the Holy Spirit, I finally passed the test that was represented by Ben, and my development in that area has continued. In fact, as I get older, I find my self more and more interested in those who are least among us, and less interested in the people I found so impressive in my youth. I actually think Lynn and I now count among our friends at least two people who have lived under a bridge at one time or another.

When we let Him, God will use our prayers to reorient our hearts. The reorientation can seem small in the beginning, but it can land us in a far, far different place as we progress along the road of life. And – thank you Lord – a far, far better place indeed.

Chapter 8

The FBI Comes to Call

In God have I put my trust; I will not be afraid what man can do unto me.
(Psalm 56:11)

It was April 14 and our personal tax return had not been filed. Even now I'm embarrassed to admit that. We were late getting our numbers together, as usual, and then were surprised to find out that our CPA had fled town for some unknown reason. With all due respect to the CPA and what appeared to be some pretty serious problems, my main concern at that point was that it was too late to find someone else and I now had to do the taxes myself. To complicate matters, I was recovering from oral surgery and had a terrible sinus headache.

So, there I sat at my desk, trying to make the numbers add up and trying to decide whether my head hurt more than my mouth, when I heard a knock at the front door.

Now, I need to digress for a moment.

Since I had begun attending my weekly Bible study, I had experienced some exciting changes in my life that I attributed to the increased level of God's Word in my spirit. I was very pleased with those changes, and I had set a goal for myself. My goal was to get so full of the Word that, no matter what life threw at me, I wouldn't panic. I hadn't expected the test of my progress to come quite so soon.

Which brings me back to the knock at the door.

I looked up from my tax work and out the window to see a well-dressed, clean-cut, 30-something-year-old man standing alone on my front porch. I picked up King, and we went to open the door together.

The man was very polite, and I immediately sensed that he didn't want to frighten me. He said he was looking for the Ourso house.

"This is one of them," I said. "Ourso families live in several of the houses back here."

"I'm looking for Sandra," he said.

"I'm Sandra," I replied, with that friendly lilt in my voice that Southerners like to use when we welcome guests to our home.

And then – it happened just like in the movies. The well-dressed, polite man reached inside his coat pocket and pulled out a black leather wallet that looked like a passport cover. As he did that one-handed flipping motion to open it for my inspection, he said, "Mrs. Ourso, I'm with the FBI, and I'm here to serve you with a subpoena to testify before a federal grand jury on April 24."

I suspect the agent is accustomed to the reaction he got. I just stood there, staring vacantly at the ominous black wallet that had FBI stenciled in letters so big that they covered the entire top half. The bottom half of the wallet held an enormous, bright gold badge that glistened in the sunlight and looked like it weighed almost as much as King – to whom I was now clinging, wondering if this might be an appropriate time for me to order him to attack.

For the record, I have led an interesting, exciting, eventful life. But it's also been an honest, law- abiding life that has not exposed me to anyone in a profession that requires a badge except for a couple of traffic cops and the security people at the airport. Nothing in my repertoire had prepared me for this.

My memory about the rest of the visit is understandably vague. Mostly, I was concentrating on trying to remember to breathe. I do know that I invited him in. And I remember wondering whether it would be appropriate to offer an FBI agent a cup of coffee.

We sat in the den and he explained to me that I was not the target of the investigation. I wasn't sure whether he was implying that I should be comforted by that fact. He said the FBI did believe, however, that I might have some information from my tenure as executive director of an agency under a previous governor that would be helpful to them.

He told me the targets. One was the agency I had headed, and the other was a man with whom I had worked. I was uncertain why the FBI would target the agency I headed but not me, but decided to let that one go for the moment in order to try to get the overall picture.

The agent said that he would like to spend a couple of hours with me prior to my grand jury testimony. I asked if I needed a lawyer. He said he couldn't advise me – that I would have to decide that for myself. Then, after we agreed that I would call him to arrange a time for our next meeting, the well-dressed, polite agent thanked me and we said a cordial goodbye.

As I watched him walk to his car, I had a very uneasy feeling. I knew I had no knowledge of any wrongdoing on my part or the part of anyone with whom I had worked. But knowing that gave me absolutely no comfort. We all know that there are people in prison who are doing the time even though they didn't do the crime. So I was finding no consolation in the fact that I wasn't a target. Besides, the fact that I wasn't a target today didn't mean that I wouldn't be tomorrow.

If ever there was a logical time to panic, this was it. But, here's the cool part. I didn't.

The moment I closed the door behind the departing FBI agent, I very calmly held that subpoena between my hands and presented the whole situation to the Lord. I assured God that I was in way over my head this time, and that He was going to have to handle the FBI.

I couldn't believe it when I heard Lynn come home, unexpectedly, about 20 minutes later. I had dreaded having to tell him about this. Lynn is one of the most spiritual people I've ever known. He depends on the Lord for everything. But he's also very emotional, and the emotional side of him frequently manifests itself first.

When he walked in, he said, "Hey. How's it goin' with the taxes?"

"Lynn," I said, "the taxes don't seem quite as important now as they did when you left for work this morning."

That one threw him. When he'd left for work that morning, I had been on the verge of hysteria about the taxes.

"Why?" he asked, looking confused.

"Because the FBI just left here," I replied, massaging my aching forehead and holding an ice pack to my swelling jaw.

"What!?!" he said, his eyes now noticeably wider. "Who were they looking for?"

"They were looking for me," I answered.

"*You*!!!!" he exclaimed in disbelief.

That's when I thought his emotional side would kick in. Instead, the second cool thing happened. He remained perfectly calm. He asked me what it was about, and I told him what little I knew. And then, bless his heart, he said, "Sandy, we need to pray."

And, boy, did we pray. We knelt together that minute and made it clear to Jesus that we were turning it all over to Him – just in case He hadn't completely understood me when I gave it to Him earlier. Then Lynn hugged me, told me not to worry, and went back to the office.

The next few weeks were not easy. The date for my testimony was pushed forward on the calendar. During that period of time, we must have gotten advice from about 100 friends, some of whom were attorneys. Without exception, they cautioned me that innocence is meaningless. Most of them told me that I was a fool if I didn't lawyer up.

Due to postponements, it took a month for all of this to evolve. During that time, I was presented with a multitude of opportunities to panic. There were times when I would wake up at night and feel the fear begin to burn in my stomach, knowing from experience that it could easily turn into searing hot terror that would soon spread out to every other inch of my body. A few times, I had to wake Lynn to get him to talk to me.

One morning, after I had awakened him for about the third time in a row, Lynn said, "Sandy, you have to stop the fear the minute you feel it begin. You have to get control of it."

I knew he was right. So the next time I woke up and felt the fear begin, I reached for my Bible and read Psalm 37. The first night, I had to read it twice before I was relaxed enough to go back to sleep. The next night, I only had to read it once. And the third night, I slept straight through until the sun came up.

Lynn and I just kept praying for God to direct us. In the end, against the advice of most of the people we consulted, I decided not to take a lawyer with me for my preliminary meeting with the FBI. I decided to rely on Jesus, in answer to our prayers, to give me the wisdom I needed in order to handle whatever came my way.

I arrived at FBI headquarters and was buzzed through a metal security door with a bulletproof glass insert. I found myself in a small room the size of a typical walk-in-closet, and saw an identical metal security door on the opposite wall. I was buzzed through the second door and greeted by the FBI agent. He escorted me into a conference room and introduced me to a federal auditor from Dallas.

The first thought that came to my mind when I sat down at the conference table was the story of Shadrach, Meshach and Abednego in the fiery furnace. And I thought, "These men think there are only three people in this conference room. But I know there are four."

Several hours of serious interrogation followed. The entire time, I sensed Jesus so close to me that I could almost feel His breath on my cheek. And I was amazed that I felt so calm and relaxed through the questioning. When we finished, the FBI agent and the auditor told me I would hear from someone in the U. S. Attorney's office after they finished their review of the boxes of files I had brought with me.

As I left FBI headquarters, I felt about the same way I had felt when I arrived. I wasn't relieved. Although I had been told in advance that I would not be allowed to tape the conversation, I found it very disturbing that the only record of the interrogation would be the agent's hand-written notes.

When we're young and naïve, we believe that truth prevails and that there is justice for the innocent. After we've been around the block a few times, we learn how life really works. And we learn how dangerous it can be to have your fate decided by mere mortals – especially when those mere mortals get paid to identify crimes and prosecute the person they believe to be the perpetrator. Even when you absolutely know you're innocent and believe that you could prove that in a court of law, the thought of the huge investment that would be required in terms of time and legal expenses can be overwhelming. The feeling of being at the mercy of that system is very much like being tied up with a thin string and then dangled out the window of a 100-story building by someone you don't know. I personally don't understand how people can handle that pressure unless they know the Lord and know that they can rely on Him to intervene.

The FBI let me dangle for a few days, and I'm sure no one will be surprised to hear that I spent a lot of that time in prayer. Ultimately, I got the call I had prayed for. An assistant U. S. Attorney informed me that they had determined that I didn't have any information about a wrongdoing, and that my testimony would not be required.

When I look back and analyze what happened, I realize how different my reaction would have been if the FBI had shown up at my door several years earlier – before I was as committed in my walk with God. What we have to be careful of, as we blitz through the over-scheduled days that make up a large percentage of our lives, is that we not ignore God when things are going well and then expect Him to show up when He hears that Nebuchadnezzar has ordered his men to stoke the fiery furnace up to seven times the heat normally used to burn human flesh – in preparation for us! Or that the FBI is at the door. Whichever.

We've been cautioned about becoming complacent. In fact, Peter clearly tells us how we must live before God our Father. "Therefore, prepare your minds for action; be self-controlled; set your hope fully on the grace to be given you when Jesus Christ is revealed. As obedient children, do not conform to the evil desires you had when you lived in ignorance. But just as he who called you is holy, so be holy in all you do; for it is written: 'Be holy, because I am holy.'" (1st Peter 1:13-16 NIV)

If our lives reflect our determination to get as close to that noble goal as we possibly can by living, to the best of our ability, within the parameters that God has set out for us in His word – not as perfect beings, which we'll never be, but as lovers of God who are consciously striving to conform to the image of His Son – we don't have to be afraid of what any man can do to us. We can go boldly before the throne of grace and plead for His mercy and His intervention.

I hope the FBI never knocks at your door. But something or someone else will. My prayer for you is that you will remember that you don't have to be in the fire alone. By your obedience to God and your commitment to holiness now, you let God know that when the fire heats up, you'll rely on Him to show up. And He will.

Chapter 9

When it Rains, it Pours

But my God shall supply all your need according to his riches
in glory by Christ Jesus.
(Philippians 4:19)

We can learn a lot about the commonality of the human experience by studying clichés. Time will tell, beauty is only skin deep, no news is good news, live and learn, what goes around comes around, haste makes waste, all is fair in love and war, beauty is as beauty does, no pain no gain, better late than never, one born every minute, what you see is what you get, no guts no glory, and, my personal favorites, the road to hell is paved with good intentions, and, the good Lord willing and the creek don't rise. That was so much fun, I could go on forever. But I don't want to bore you to death.

Since I'm a human being, you'll not be surprised to hear that certain periods of my life can be summarized by clichés. The period I'd currently like to address could best be described as the money-doesn't-grow-on-trees period – a time that can easily be distinguished from the rolling-in-the-dough phase of my life.

I need to lay some groundwork. Lynn and I each made more than enough money when we were single. Then, when we married and pooled our resources, we had possessions aplenty and lots of spare money. Neither of us had ever borrowed money, except to finance a house or an occasional car, nor had we ever carried a balance on a credit card. We had, shall we say, led financially sheltered lives.

The decision for me to quit work to stay at home after our baby was born was an important one. My paycheck was substantial, so the monetary hit was significant. But we were willing to give up some of our more extravagant habits, and felt secure that we had adequate savings to cover unexpected expenses for a number of years.

Don't you just know that God must laugh when He hears us making long-range plans?

So here we were, five and one-half years after I had quit work, and life decided to bombard us with some very significant, unanticipated financial dilemmas. Consequently, I was experiencing the kind of pressure that is produced by not having enough money.

One morning after my 33rd review of the situation, I realized that I wasn't going to be able to come up with the answer. No matter how creatively I approached the subject, the numbers simply refused to break my way. So, confident that I was at the end of my personal rope, I ran to God and prayed for His direction.

When I finished praying, I turned on the TV. Before I could change the channel, I heard a man say that he had decided to go register at a university on faith, despite the fact that he didn't have any money, because he was confident that God wanted him to do this and, therefore, that God would miraculously provide the funds. The problem, he said, was that he actually got as far as the front of the line to pay his registration fee, and he still didn't have any money. The clerk told him how much it would be, and was staring at him, waiting for him to write a check. But he knew he couldn't. There was no money in the account.

At that point, he said he felt the Holy Spirit leading him to call his father.

"I didn't know why I was supposed to call my dad," he said, "because I had no intention of asking him for the money. But I knew I was supposed to call him."

So, he excused himself from the line and called his parents' house. As soon as he got his daddy on the phone, his daddy said, "Son, where have you been!? I've been trying to find you. Mr. Smith had a check for you, so he asked me to take it to the bank and deposit it in your account." The amount of the check was the exact amount that this man needed to pay his registration fee.

I wondered if there was supposed to be a message in any of this for me. I knew I could call my father and get whatever money I needed, but I had no intention of doing that. However, I'm accustomed to direction coming when I need it, sometimes from unlikely sources, so I decided to pray about what I had just heard. "Lord," I said, "if you want the money to come from Daddy, then I need you to have him call me."

Now, you have to know my father to understand the remoteness of that possibility. Daddy spent many years working for the local power company as manager of the service department – a job that required him to be on call 24/7. He often got calls when he was at home, all hours of the day or night. Many of the calls concerned problems that he could handle on the phone. But sometimes those calls meant he had to go to the office. On some occasions, due to persistent severe weather, we didn't see him again for several days. Being a slave to the phone all those years had given him a unique perspective on telephones. It might best be described as an aversion bordering on phobia.

In addition to his aversion to the telephone, it simply wasn't necessary for him to call in order to keep in touch with me because I called my parents fairly often. Since we lived at opposite ends of the state and didn't see each other frequently, Mother and I emailed often and I usually called them every week or so. For these reasons,

I doubt that Daddy had called me more than three or four times in the entire seven years I had lived in Baton Rouge.

About 11:30 that morning, I decided to get on my treadmill to see if a little exercise might at least help me work off some stress. The treadmill was in my bedroom. We keep the ringer on the telephone turned off so the phone won't bother us when we're sleeping. The answering machine is always on, screening calls, and I rarely answer the phone before I know who is calling.

I had been on the treadmill for about 20 minutes, and was watching the news on TV. The TV was turned up pretty loud so I could hear over the noise of the treadmill motor. But I thought I heard the answering machine click. When Caroline is in school, I like to check my messages as quickly as possible in case there's an emergency.

I got off the treadmill, walked over to the answering machine and pushed the "play" button. I was astonished to hear my dad's voice.

He said, "Sandy, I have some money I had planned to give you next time you and Caroline are here. If it's gonna be a while, let me know and I'll send it to you."

I stood there for a moment, in quiet amazement.

When I returned Daddy's call, he told me the amount. It was exactly what I needed. Daddy was surprised when I started crying. I doubt that he's ever given anything to anyone that prompted quite so strong a reaction.

As difficult as it can be to stand in faith, out on the limb of desperation and uncertainty, I wouldn't trade those experiences for any amount of security that comes from my own ability. It was wonderful that I could, for most of my life, write a check for anything I wanted, any time I wanted it. But few things in life are as exciting as being at the end of your own abilities, and having God come through in a dramatic and miraculous way.

I am genuinely grateful to God for the opportunities I've had to rest in the warmth of His love when He reaches down to meet my needs, and for the strengthening of my faith that has followed each of those times. At the end of the rope doesn't sound like a good place to be. But if that's where we can best experience God's love for us, then it's absolutely the most blessed place in the universe.

A friend of mine once said to me, "I believe in God, but I don't love Him the way you do." I've thought about that a lot. And the answer I keep going back to is that He was not only willing to hang on a cross for me, but He has walked down so many difficult roads with me in my life. He's the one I run to when I'm in a tight spot, and I think I may have been in more than the average number of tight spots. He has rescued me so many times. He has so often been my only hope when I absolutely knew that I couldn't help myself.

I almost feel sorry for people who have waltzed through easy lives, getting all the breaks, always having enough money or power or influence or luck to fix everything that looks like it might block their path. They don't need to run to God and cry out to him. They can fix it themselves – or they know someone who can. Unfortunately, that doesn't build intimacy with God. Relationship comes from interaction, and love grows when you watch Jesus, time after time, help you despite the fact that you know you are absolutely the least deserving person on the entire planet.

If you're in one of those end-of-your-rope places in your life, be grateful for everything just the way it is right now. It can be one of the greatest blessings in your life. All you have to do is recognize it as an opportunity to run to God and get close to Him and build intimacy with Him. He loves you. And He wants you to ask Him for help.

Chapter 10

The Leading of a Patient Parent

*But you are a forgiving God, gracious and compassionate,
slow to anger and abounding in love.*
(Nehemiah 9:17b NIV)

A s is the case with some women when they become a mothers, the birth of my child caused my entire brain to radically reorder itself – much like a kaleidoscope occasionally does with just a slight turn. Among the things that had seemed insignificant before, but suddenly became earth shatteringly important, was the fact that my husband and I were not of the same denomination.

So, I set about to rectify that little problem. My thinking on the subject went something like this. Because we live in the town in which my husband was born and reared, and because his very large extended family is deeply entrenched and highly visible in their denomination, it appeared that the logical course of action was for me to affiliate with his church. It started out as a purely intellectual decision, but the year-long conversion process ended up being one of the most significant spiritual experiences of my life. The details of that story are worth telling – but for another time.

My primary concern about my new denomination was the lack of opportunities for Bible study that had been such an integral part of my experience in my former denomination. So I began looking for a Bible study that could supplement what I was getting from the Church. I found one, joined, and participated with great enthusiasm for five years.

The time came when it was impossible for me to continue in that study. I dropped out, and I missed it terribly.

After almost a year of no formal Bible study, I began praying that God would lead me to another. The former study was an outstanding international, non-denominational study attended by 500+ women in my community, and the likelihood that I would find another of that caliber was slim. But I had finally caught on to the fact that I didn't need to have all the answers. I just needed to pray and ask God to help me.

After a few months of praying, I saw a friend from the old Bible study in a restaurant one Sunday afternoon. I told her how much I missed the study and that I was looking for another. She told me that she had some friends in our denomination who were starting a study. She didn't know much about it, but thought they were meeting in someone's home. She said she'd check and see if they would be willing for someone they didn't know to join them, and she'd let me know. When I never heard from her, I assumed that the group preferred to keep the study private. I didn't want to risk putting her in an embarrassing position, so I decided not to call her to follow up.

Fast-forward several *more* months – and I was *still* praying about this. By then I had become a little frustrated, and one night during my prayers I said to God, with greater emphasis than usual, "God you *know* how much I want to be in another Bible study! I *need* you to lead me to one!!"

The next day, Lynn and I were in a different restaurant, and ran into the same friend. As the conversation ensued, it became apparent to me that she had simply forgotten about our previous conversation. She mentioned the Bible study again, told me that the group had decided to hold their meetings at a church, that the name of the lecture leader was Judy, and suggested that I go check it out. At the risk of sounding neurotic, I hesitated to make the contact because I didn't know whether the study organizers might want this particular study to be for their church members only. So I kept praying – kept stressing to God that I needed an answer.

A few days passed and I was still stewing over this. I was wondering how to proceed one afternoon when I did what I frequently do in a crisis. I turned on the TV. Before I had a chance to change the channel, I heard a man address the woman sitting next to him as Judy. That grabbed my attention. Judy was the name of the Bible study lecture leader that my friend had mentioned to me. I started listening and, to my absolute amazement, I realized that it was the Judy from the Bible study. In fact, she was being interviewed about the Bible study and, in the process, answered all of my questions and settled my concerns about whether I would be welcome.

By this time, I think God had realized that I was being unusually obtuse and that He needed to make sure I got the message.

So, the following Sunday, as I sat in church waiting for the service to begin, I looked up from praying just in time to see the Judy from the TV show, a woman I'd never seen before in my life until I saw her on TV the previous week, walk in and sit down in the pew right in front of me!

I was appropriately astounded.

After church, I stopped Judy and told her the whole story and got the details about dates and times. The day and time worked perfectly for me, and I joined that Bible study the very next week.

I think this example is such a marvelous illustration of how God works to answer our prayers about routine issues, how we have to cooperate with Him, and also of God's patience. He started dropping clues in front of me immediately, but I didn't adequately follow up with my part of the activity. Why would I have hesitated when I heard about the Bible study the first time? I knew I was praying to a prayer-answering God. I should have recognized the potential answer and sought information more aggressively instead of waiting for someone to call me.

But the most amazing part is how our patient Lord didn't give up on me. He just kept lovingly sending me hints, trying to guide me into my answer, even while I accused Him of ignoring my plea.

That patience is such a wonderful example for us as parents. The way we parents think the system is supposed to work is that we tell our kids something one time and they understand and incorporate what we said and then – praise God – we never have to cover that territory again. We want to quickly cram information down their tiny throats and into their developing brains, and we get annoyed if a subject comes up a second time. How nice that God doesn't treat us that way.

I will be eternally grateful to God for leading me into a Bible study that meets my needs, fits my schedule, and has served to introduce me to some of the most amazing women of God that I've ever met. I'm even more grateful that He loved me enough to be patient with me despite my failure to follow up on His obvious leading. And I know that there is one very effective way that I can show my gratitude to God for that loving kindness. I can react with loving kindness to that growing-up version of the baby girl who caused my brain to reorder itself – even when she doesn't react the way I think she should every time. I suspect that one of the things that causes God's heart to sing is watching us when we imitate Him in our loving and kind and patient approach in our dealings with the precious children that He has entrusted into our care.

So, go surprise your kids. Treat them with kindness and patience. It is from watching how you conduct yourself that they will learn that God is a forgiving God, gracious and compassionate, slow to anger and abounding in love.

Chapter 11

His Ways are Higher Than Our Ways

For my thoughts are not your thoughts, neither are your ways my ways,
saith the Lord. For as the heavens are higher than the earth, so are my
ways higher than your ways, and my thoughts than your thoughts.
(Isaiah 55:8,9)

"Lord, lead me to a tape that will help her," I prayed as
I ran through the light rain that had blown in with the
afternoon thunderstorm. I continued to pray as I walked through
the front door of the huge, well-stocked and brightly illuminated
Christian bookstore. "She needs help so badly, Lord. Please help

me find the kind of music she will enjoy with lyrics that will speak to her heart."

I had just hung up from talking with my sister, Kathy, who was still in Mississippi. According to her account, she and Steve had fought (Yes, again!) a few days before. Not known as a particularly cool head, Kathy had reacted by smashing her fist through a window. I just happened to call the day after she got her arm stitched up, and heard her despondent account of this latest episode. She was frightened, and talked of having almost bled to death on the way to the hospital.

I had tried to get her to leave him. But I knew all too well that she would leave that mess when she was ready and that there was nothing I could do to shorten the timetable. One way I had been able to help, however, was to continue to make her the subject of prayer every week when I met with my three prayer partners.

All of this was on my mind when I entered the bookstore. I had boxed up some little things to send to Kathy, hoping to give her a few moments of pleasure when she opened the package. But I wanted to include some music before I sealed the box.

Kathy and I shared a love for music – primarily the hard rock and Southern rock of the late '60s and early '70s. But I thought Christian music would be the best choice for her based on her current predicament. Since I really knew very little about Christian artists, I was relying on God to help me with my selection.

"Please show me, Lord," my prayer continued. "Show me what will help her."

As I walked through the store, I approached what looked like the longest wall I'd ever seen in my life. It was lined with thousands of music tapes, stacked from floor to ceiling. For someone who knew nothing about Christian artists, it was overwhelming. "I have no idea where to begin," I prayed as I stared at the wall in disbelief. "Help me, Lord."

As I slowly approached the wall of tapes, continuing to pray for help, all of the tapes on the wall began to blur – almost as though I were viewing them through fog or rising steam. As I walked closer, trying to figure out what was wrong with my eyes, I realized that one tape on the shelves was still in focus.

I got all the way up to the shelves, and reached toward that one tape. I looked at the cover, and was surprised and delighted to see a name I recognized; B. J. Thomas. I knew him. He certainly wasn't a hard-rock kind of guy, but I knew his work, and knew that his image was one that would be acceptable to my sister. The songs listed were old standards, but I knew I could rely on B. J. Thomas to merge the old with a little more modern style that would interest a younger, hipper listener. It wouldn't be rock 'n roll, but it just might be close enough.

I was thrilled. God had shown me which tape to buy. "Thank you, Lord," I prayed as I paid for the tape. "Thank you for sure and swift guidance to music that I know will help Kathy at a time when she needs help so very badly."

I practically ran to my car as I peeled the cellophane from the plastic cassette box. I pushed the tape into my tape player as I backed out of my parking space, and turned up the volume. I was prepared for the music that the Lord, in His wisdom, had led me to that would help my sister into a better frame of mind!

The drive home was a short one, and I was eager to hear as much of the tape as possible during the ride. As I fast-forwarded from one cut to the next, disappointment began to settle over me like a heavy blanket. This was wrong. This wasn't the B. J. Thomas I had expected to hear. These songs were done in a slow, traditional style that would be more appropriate for my mother. Or my grandmother!

My confusion grew with my disappointment as I reached the end of the tape. I had asked God to guide me. I had depended on Him because I knew nothing about Christian artists. He knew how desperately I wanted to help my sister, and how little there was that I could do other than this. But this tape was wrong. Kathy would never relate to this.

"Why, Lord?" I cried as I drove toward home. "I needed You and so completely trusted You to make this selection for me? Why? And why did all the other tapes blur except this one? What was that all about?"

By the time I pulled into my driveway, the elation I had felt in the store had completely evaporated. I was frustrated and confused and disappointed and so very, very hurt.

I walked into my house and picked up the box I was planning to mail to my sister. I had been waiting to mail it until I could include the right music. But it needed to go now. The right music would just have to wait.

As I started to seal the carton, I looked over at the B. J. Thomas tape I had disgustedly tossed onto the desk. I knew it wasn't what she needed, but I certainly didn't want the stupid thing lying around my house. At least Kathy would see that I had made the effort.

So, I threw the tape in, sealed the carton, and took my inadequate little package to the post office.

As I left the post office, I tried to put the whole thing out of my mind. I didn't understand any of what had happened, but I knew I needed to get over my disappointment. I hadn't been traveling in Christian circles very long, but it had been long enough for me to hear a lot of people talk about us not understanding God's ways. Well, they were right about that one! I didn't understand.

Several days passed before I heard from Kathy. She called to thank me for the package, and talked about several of the little items I had enclosed that had made her smile.

"But most of all," she said, "I want to thank you for the tape. The songs were so soothing and so relaxing. I've listened to it over and over. It calms me and has helped me more than anything. It was just what I needed."

I'm sure there was more to the conversation, but I don't really remember. The only thing I remember is sitting on the sofa in my den, in breathless silence, with the telephone still in my hand.

And I remember crying. I was overwhelmed with gratitude. But I was also heartbroken by the realization that our ignorance so often obscures our view when it comes to the efforts that our merciful God makes on our behalf.

I reflect on the incident of the B. J. Thomas tape when my faith is low and the answers to prayer don't seem to be flowing as quickly. And I remind myself that sometimes, when we believe God hasn't come through for us, we may just be forgetting how much higher God's ways are than our own.

Chapter 12

He Knows My Name

But the very hairs of your head are all numbered. (Matthew 10:30)

For the first time in a number of administrations, we had no connections with the governor of the state.

It was a strange feeling, actually, not knowing the people who lived in the Governor's Mansion. My husband's family had lived in six of the houses that make up the little subdivision adjoining the mansion property since the 1960s, and someone in the family had always had some sort of connection with the governor's family.

But now, for the first time, none of us had ever even met this newly elected man.

This was especially frustrating in light of the fact that we had a problem that we believed could only be solved by the governor. Since none of the traditional channels were going to work for us, we were in the process of figuring out which, if any, of our acquaintances had influence with this man who had moved to the capitol city from the opposite side of the state.

This situation was weighing heavily on my mind one warm summer day as I walked along our neighborhood street with four-year-old Caroline. She was picking up rocks and examining leaves and pulling up grass while I talked to God about how in the world we would be able to get through to this man with whom we had no entrée.

As we walked and played, just a few yards from the back door of the Governor's Mansion, Caroline began singing one of my favorite songs that she had learned at mother's day out:

"God is so good,

"God is so good,

"God is so good,

"He's so good to me," she sang.

"How are we supposed to reach the governor?" I asked God, as I sauntered along at a pace that was acceptable to a curious four-year-old, watching her stop at every intriguing rock that lay in her path, listening to her continue to sing.

"Lord, only the governor has the power over this agency. Only he can order them to do what needs to be done to right this terrible wrong," I prayed.

Caroline continued singing in her engaging little baby voice:

"He loves me so,

"He loves me so,

"He loves me so,

"He's so good to me."

"How simple this would be," I thought, as I stared at the back of the mansion while Caroline threw rocks into the storm drain, "if Lynn and I knew this governor, as we had known governors before, and could just schedule a time to drop by the mansion and explain how we need his help.

"But this governor doesn't even know us," I thought. "He doesn't even know our names."

Caroline continued singing:

"He knows my name,

"He knows my name,"

I turned and stared at Caroline in disbelief as she continued that last verse.

"He knows my name,

"He's so good to me."

"He knows my name!" I thought. "My heavens. Here I am, concentrating on the governor, and my daughter is singing about the Creator of the Universe. The Creator of the Universe knows my name."

I was shocked that she had sung that verse at precisely the right moment. And I immediately recognized how wrong my focus had been.

"Here I am," I thought, "worrying about the fact that one little governor of one little state in this one little country on this one little planet in this one little galaxy doesn't know my name. Instead, I should be dwelling on the fact that the Creator of the Universe, who spoke all of creation into being, *does* know my name. He not only knows my name, but He is so concerned about me that He has counted all the hairs on my head! And, as He has proven in so many times past, He is willing to intervene on my behalf."

I started laughing – and I continued to laugh at myself for the smallness of thinking that is the inevitable consequence of assuming that I'm supposed to figure out these things on my own. From time to time, we all find ourselves reverting to the place where we think we have to figure out how it's all supposed to work, and then we eagerly run to inform God what we've concluded. We don't actually state it this way, but what we're really saying is, "OK, God. I've thought this through and I've got it worked out. This is what you need to do." Then we proceed to give Him directions.

Does it get any more absurd than that?

So I stopped trying to figure it out and I prayed. I asked God for His help with the situation that I had thought only the governor could handle. Then I started looking for rocks with my daughter, and I never spent another moment worrying about the situation. I had turned it all over to Jesus.

The problem with the agency was never resolved the way we had hoped. But as more time passes, I've begun to realize that if we had been able to convince the governor to do what we wanted, things would not have worked out well in the long run.

What a surprise! We didn't have the answer after all.

We don't know the future. Neither does the governor. But God does. I don't know about you, but I'd prefer to have my fate in the hands of one who knows the future, knows how things need to happen in order to serve the best interest of everyone involved, is so concerned about me that He has counted the hairs on my head, and isn't worried about reelection or about keeping His major contributors happy.

The best part of all is that God isn't locked away in a mansion, unavailable unless we know the right people. He is always there for us. All we have to do is call on His name, any time, day or night, from any location. And He doesn't need our instructions.

I have actually found that the simpler my prayer, the less likely it is that I'm trying to run the show and give God directions. I learned that from another little child.

One day I was watching a TV talk show that is hosted by an evangelist and his wife. They usually have an interesting guest who is interviewed by the evangelist, who talks a lot. The evangelist's wife sits beside him and rarely has anything to add. On this particular day, however, she wanted to tell a story.

She said that on one occasion she was not feeling well, and called her daughter to ask for prayer. The daughter's very young son answered the phone. The woman said to her little grandson, "Honey, Mimi doesn't feel well. I need you to pray for me." To that, the child immediately replied, "Jesus! Mimi!"

I will never forget that story. I think that prayer is one of the most profound I've ever heard, and the older I get the more I use that prayer myself. The older I get, the more I realize that we just don't know much of anything! We know that we're supposed to pray for a person's salvation or safety or healing. But when we get into more complicated issues, we're better off most of the time to just bring that person to God's attention and let Him figure out what needs to be done.

The present governor knows our names. But I'm not feeling the need for that nearly as much as I once did. I figure we're better off just going straight to the top. In the long run, I think we're better off working with someone who is so concerned about us that He has gone to the trouble of counting the hairs on our heads.

Chapter 13

The Prayer of Jehoshaphat

"Oh our God, will you not judge them? For we have no power to face this vast army that is attacking us. We do not know what to do, but our eyes are upon you." (II Chronicles 20:12 NIV)

O f all the examples of heartfelt and answered prayer I've heard in my life, one of my favorites is in the story of King Jehoshaphat. I consider Jehoshaphat's handling of the crisis that was about to befall his kingdom to be a model of the way a mature Christian should approach all problems, great or small.

Following the death in 873 B.C. of his father, Asa, 35-year-old Jehoshaphat rose to the throne and ruled in Judah as a righteous king whose heart was lifted up to the ways of the Lord. Despite living the royal life of great wealth and power in Jerusalem, Jehoshaphat never became vain or prideful. Instead, he worked hard to rid his kingdom of idolatry and to see that his people were educated in the Law of God. He appointed righteous judges across the land, and warned them to fear the Lord and act carefully. "Act firmly," he told them, "and the Lord will be with the good."

At some point – probably just about the time Jehoshaphat began feeling full of confidence and basking in self-congratulations over having done such a superb job as a kingdom administrator – things took a sudden turn. A message arrived that a coalition of Transjordanian armies was coming against him from south of the Dead Sea, moving north near the western shore. Despite the fact that he had a standing army of 1,160,000 men, news of the much greater number coming against him frightened Jehoshaphat. Then the Bible reports that he "...hastened to consult the Lord."

Now that's impressive. He didn't immediately get on a conference call with his two best friends and weep and moan about life being unfair and about how he didn't deserve it and how awful it was going to be for the people and how could God let this happen to him when he'd done *nothing* except serve faithfully. The good king understood that his faithfulness didn't exempt him from the threat of trouble. Time spent grumbling and murmuring would be time wasted.

The next move Jehoshaphat made was equally impressive. He took action that would immediately draw God into the fray. He proclaimed a fast for all inhabitants of the land of Judah, and the people from every one of the cities came to Jerusalem to seek guidance from the Lord.

I recently heard a noted Bible teacher discuss the subject of fasting. He said that any time he's faced with a significant issue and doesn't know what to do, he declares a three-day fast and spends his time praying for God's guidance. He said that he rarely gets through the third day without receiving direction.

Next, the Bible reports that Jehoshaphat stood up in the assembly in the house of the Lord and prayed. Here's what he said:

"O Lord, God of our fathers, are you not the God who is in heaven? You rule over all the kingdoms of the nations. Power and might are in your hand, and no one can withstand you. O our God, did you not drive out the inhabitants of this land before your people Israel and give it forever to the descendants of Abraham your friend? They have lived in it and built in it a sanctuary for your Name, saying, 'If calamity comes upon us, whether the sword of judgment, or plague or famine, we will stand in your presence before this temple that bears your Name and will cry out to you in our distress, and you will hear us and save us.'" (II Chronicles 20:6-9 NIV)

Of course, Jehoshaphat isn't really asking God if He's in heaven, and he isn't telling God anything he thinks God doesn't already know. He's reminding himself, and the people who are listening, of who God is, what He has done for them in the past, and the promises He has made to the people regarding the future. And he's reminding the people of the decision they made in calmer times about how they would handle a crisis when it arose. He knows that their faith needs to be increased to the point of boldness in the face of this hopeless situation.

We can do the same thing. When trouble strikes (notice I say *when* not *if*) in our own lives, we need to rehearse the promises of God that are in the Bible and call to mind the times that He has rescued the heroes of our faith, and us, in the past. That builds our faith – causes it to puff up in preparation to meet what's coming against us. We also need to fall back on a preconceived game plan – something we've formulated during the calm between the storms. Salesmen say, "Plan your work and work your plan." That is never more important than when we're talking about a plan for how we're going to discipline ourselves to walk in God's ways during a crisis.

Jehoshaphat continues: "But now here are men from Ammon, Moab and Mount Seir, whose territory you would not allow Israel to invade when they came from Egypt; so they turned away from them and did not destroy them. See how they are repaying us by coming to drive us out of the possession you gave us as an inheritance." (II Chronicles 20:10-11 NIV)

Here, the king reminds God that their hands are clean – that his people have not done anything to provoke this action that is coming against them. They have only followed God's instructions in the way that they have reacted to these people in the past.

Now the king has succinctly summarized to God the problem they are currently facing. And then comes my very favorite part.

"O our God, will you not judge them? For we have no power to face this vast army that is attacking us. We do not know what to do, but our eyes are upon you." (II Chronicles 20:12 NIV)

And then, everyone from Judah just stood before the Lord – the men and their wives and their children. They just stood there.

Every time I read this passage in the Bible, I'm struck by Jehoshaphat's humility. Kings tend to be macho guys who want to appear to have all the answers. If a king doesn't have the answers, then he usually likes to confer privately with his faithful advisors. Under threat of beheading, the underlings usually manage to come up with a brilliant solution that the king can take credit for himself. I have not read about many kings in my life who were willing to quickly mount the podium and declare for all the world to hear that they don't have a clue what to do next. But that's what Jehoshaphat did. He declared himself powerless, said he didn't know what to do, and then he just stood before God with all the rest of the regular people in the kingdom.

If one of the greatest kings in history can say he's powerless and doesn't have a clue, surely it's OK for us to say that. One of the most comforting things my husband can say to me in a time of crisis is, "I don't know what to do." My heart sings when I hear him say that. When he admits that he doesn't know what to do, I know that he will pray for God to direct him. And that knowledge is the one thing that will immediately cause my spirit to calm down and move into a more peaceful place.

The mistake most of us make is that we think we have to do something. I've heard people say, "Do something, even if you do it wrong!" That's the American way. Take action! Take the bull by the horns! Pull yourself up by your bootstraps! Don't just sit there. Do something – anything! We equate waiting with laziness and indecision. We want to at least get on the phone and give somebody a piece of our mind!

But there's a better way. It's a harder way because it requires more discipline than shooting from the hip. The better way is to fast and pray for God's guidance, and then wait to hear from Him.

I'm not, of course, recommending this as a course of action when your shoestrings come untied. If your shoestrings come untied, tie them. There are times when we know what to do. But, when you're between the proverbial rock and a hard place and don't have absolute confidence in any of the brilliant schemes that are racing through your head, then fast and pray and wait on God.

The story of Jehoshaphat continues as the Spirit of the Lord comes on Jahaziel, a Levite. He said, "Listen, King Jehoshaphat and all who live in Judah and Jerusalem! This is what the Lord says to you: 'Do not be afraid or discouraged because of this vast army. For the battle is not yours, but God's. Tomorrow march down against them. They will be climbing up by the Pass of Ziz, and you will find them at the end of the gorge in the Desert of Jeruel. You will not have to fight this battle. Take up your positions; stand firm and see the deliverance the Lord will give you. O Judah and Jerusalem. Do not be afraid; do not be discouraged. Go out to face them tomorrow, and the Lord will be with you.'" (II Chronicles 20:15-17 NIV)

Then Jehoshaphat and all his people fell down before the Lord in worship, and Levites rose to sing praises to the God of Israel in a resounding chorus.

What a glorious sight that must have been. I've known that feeling – the feeling that comes when you know God has come through with the answer you so desperately needed. There's no better feeling in the world – and it will cause you to fall down before God. My heart breaks for people who are so self-sufficient that they've never been in a situation where their resources have run out and their only recourse is to cry out to God for help. They truly don't know what they're missing – not knowing what it's like to have God come through in the midst of the impossible.

No matter what our economic level, we tend to look at those in the level above us with envy. Instead, we should recognize that material possessions are so often a hindrance to an intimate relationship with God. Self-sufficiency frequently keeps us propped up, preventing us from falling on our faces before Him.

Another point to bring out here is that, as wonderful as it was to get a word from God, the word didn't make sense. I mean, look at what God said. He said they wouldn't have to fight. When you've got an army coming against you that is so huge that your army of 1,160,000 looks uselessly puny, it's a little difficult to believe that it won't be necessary to do any fighting. But that's what God said. He said they wouldn't have to fight. It reminds me of how many times in my life a word from God has been so completely opposite of anything I would have considered to be a likely solution.

Back to Jehoshaphat. I picture this next part in my vivid imagination every time I read the story. It's always the same – much like a scene from a Mel Gibson movie. It's early the next morning, and the multitude has now moved out into the wilderness to get in formation for the march toward the enemy. Jehoshaphat is standing on a high place, yelling in order to be heard by as many people as possible.

"Listen to me, O people of Judah and Jerusalem!" he said. "Believe in the Lord, your God, and you shall have success! Believe his prophets, and everything will be all right." (II Chronicles 20:20b TLB)

Then, after talking with some of the people, the king made a decision that may have caused concern among even the most confident. He appointed *singers* to march in *front of the army* singing praises to the Lord. As the group marched forward, *having been ordered not to fight*, the singers broke into, "Give thanks to the Lord, for his mercy endures forever."

Now that, my friends, is not a battle plan that either Patton or Rommel would have agreed to go along with.

This dramatic scene always makes me think of Joshua at the battle of Jericho. I suspect the people found it a little disconcerting when Joshua informed them that the battle plan was to defeat Jericho by marching around it while blowing horns and yelling. I've said it before, but it bears repeating. What God tells you to do will frequently not line up with anything that makes sense to your rational mind. That's part of the test. The idea is to trust Him enough to do it anyway.

One of my favorite illustrations of this was told by a South Louisiana preacher who was somewhere in the North preaching a revival. He had agreed to have dinner with one of the church families, at the invitation of the wife, who said she was cooking gumbo. As it turns out, the woman's husband did not attend church and was not happy about having a preacher at his house for dinner. The preacher sat down at the dinner table, across from the husband who made no attempt to appear hospitable, and took the first bite of the worst gumbo he had ever tasted in his life.

As the preacher sat there, gumbo in mouth, husband glaring at him and wife eagerly anticipating a compliment, he distinctly heard the Lord say, "Tell her it's awful." Spoon still suspended in the air, the preacher's panic began to grow as he silently begged God not to make him do that – that it was crazy. He begged, "God, please just let me tell her it's fine." God said, "No. Tell her it's awful."

So the horrified preacher forced himself to swallow and, bracing himself for the explosion that he was confident would follow, said, "Lady, that's the worst gumbo I've ever tasted."

He said the husband instantly jumped up and threw his spoon down. The preacher said he knew beyond a doubt that the man was about to beat him to a pulp.

Then the husband said, "Every preacher who has ever been to this house to eat gumbo has told my wife it was wonderful. You're the only preacher who has ever come here and told the truth about this horrible gumbo."

The next night, the husband came to church to hear the only honest preacher he'd ever met.

At the risk of repeating myself too many times, sometimes what God tells you to do won't make sense – things like putting singers at the front of the army, or telling people you don't like their gumbo.

The good news is that Jehoshaphat was vindicated just as quickly as the South Louisiana preacher. Because, *at the very moment that Jehoshaphat's singers began singing*, the enemy soldiers began to kill one another. And when the people of Judah came to the watchtower of the desert and looked toward the enemy, they saw nothing but corpses littering the ground. The enemy had continued to fight among themselves until they had totally wiped themselves out. There were no survivors.

The moment the people of Judah began to praise God, they had the victory. They didn't know it until they reached the scene and saw the bodies. But before they even started their march, they had won the war. And that's often true with us. The victory often has occurred for some period of time before we see it with our own eyes. The important part is for us to exercise the necessary discipline to keep the praises going – to keep singing praises to God until the victory manifests itself in the natural realm.

King Jehoshaphat's obedience to God in this situation had long-ranging effects on the kingdom. His men took so much plunder from the dead soldiers – cattle, personal property, garments and precious vessels – that it took them three days to gather everything. When word of this great victory spread to the surrounding lands, the fear of God settled on all the kingdoms, and "…the kingdom of Jehoshaphat was at peace, for his God had given him rest on every side." (II Chronicles 20:30 NIV) Jehoshaphat reigned in peace for 25 years, and was eventually buried with his distinguished ancestors in the City of David.

Like asking for directions when we're lost, admitting that we don't know what to do in times of crisis can be more difficult for some personality types than for others. Some people are dependent by nature, and relying on God is easy for them. Others have problems with pride and ego that have to be overcome before they can move into a walk of true dependence on God. But, whatever it takes, we have to master this. We're all king of something. If you have children, you're a king. If you have a job, you're a king. We may not have as many subjects as Jehoshaphat, but God has put all of us in a position of authority over someone or something. In order to rule and reign responsibly, we all must do the work that is necessary to reduce ourselves to the point of dependence on God.

Ultimately, no matter what our kingdom encounters, our hope is in the Lord. The battle is His. We just have to be bold and coura-geous and responsible and humble enough to fall on our faces before God and beg for His help.

And then, don't just do something! Sit there!

Chapter 14

My Friend Michelle

I lift up my eyes to the hills – where does my help come from? My help comes from the Lord, the Maker of heaven and earth.
(Psalms 121: 1-2 NIV)

Michelle grew up a child of privilege, living the American dream in the lush, green beauty of Baton Rouge, Louisiana. She was the daughter of a vivacious and devoted mom, and a brilliant father whose engineering firm was financially successful and highly respected. Michelle and her three younger brothers went to the best schools and summer camps, and belonged to all the right clubs. As their family grew and needed more space, Michelle's parents built one of the first homes on Pikes Lane – a premier location in our city – when it was still a gravel road surrounded by woods and vacant fields.

Life couldn't have been better for Michelle and her family. Until the day the walls came tumbling down.

It was Mardi Gras day, and Michelle was 11 years old. Her best friend, Mary Kay, rode her bike from two streets over that morning and ran into Michelle's room to wake her. Just as Michelle began to try to open her eyes and move toward consciousness, she said something that neither of them understood at that moment.

"I told Mary Kay that I had seen my daddy – that he was sitting in a rocker in the corner of my room. The rocker wasn't on the floor. It was in the air. And Daddy told me he was OK. Then I repeated the verse that he had said to me:

'Do you see me in the corner,
Do you see me rocking in the chair up there?
I'll tell you of my life and all the dreams it holds,
I am where there is no darkness.'"

The two preteens were puzzled by what had just happened. But they dismissed it as just a weird dream, and Michelle managed to ignore the strange feeling. After all, her father couldn't possibly have been in her room. He wasn't even in town. He had flown out a few days earlier in a private plane with three other engineers, and they weren't scheduled to be back from their business trip until later in the day.

Michelle got dressed, and the two young friends jumped on their bikes and headed for Mary Kay's house on Peggy Street. They spent part of the day shopping for shoes, and then went back to Mary Kay's to bake cookies.

"We had only been home for a while when my Aunt Bonnie called me and told me to come home immediately," said Michelle.

Michelle rode her bike home. When she walked into the house, family members were there, crying. Michelle was about to find out that the private plane carrying her beloved father and the other engineers had crashed. There were no survivors.

"They told me Daddy was dead," said Michelle. "They told me he had gone to heaven."

Her father's death began a long period of very difficult years in which Michelle fought to regain her emotional equilibrium. She would go outside for long walks alone at night because the house seemed so suffocating she couldn't bear to be inside. Her father had loved Jesus with all his heart, and young Michelle struggled to resist the notion that he had died because, as he had often said, he wanted to be in heaven with Jesus. For years after her father was buried, Michelle hated the smell of "funeral flowers." She clung to her paternal grandparents, Mimi and Deedee, because they were a tangible part of her father. Being with them helped her cope with the gaping, dark void that nothing could fill.

Three years after her father's death, Michelle's mother, Jodie, began dating Tommy, a local lawyer whose wife, Bootsie, had died of breast cancer. On her deathbed, Bootsie had told Tommy she wanted him to marry Jodie. I've often marveled at the unselfishness of a woman who would spend her final hours thinking about a new wife for her grieving husband and a mother for their devastated children. Part of Bootsie's miracle of selflessness is that Tommy and Jodie fell in love and married.

The fused family would spend the next few years working out their heartaches and differences while the two overwhelmed but loving parents tried to maintain the appearance that they were in charge. The dozen of them lived in a three-story showplace designed by A. Hayes Town, the premier South Louisiana architect, which was secluded from view on a wooded lot just outside the city limits. Jodie had a retired priest come to the house every Sunday to make sure that all the kids, even the ones who might prefer to sneak off instead of going to Mass, received Communion.

Mimi and Deedee continued to provide Michelle with love and support. Her devotion to her Mimi, who was a great cook, plus the geographic good luck of being born in food-obsessed South Louisiana, were responsible for Michelle's passion for cooking.

And it was that passion that eventually landed her at the LaVarenne Culinary Institution in the heart of Paris.

Michelle returned to South Louisiana as an accomplished culinary professional, and quickly established a successful catering business of her own. She had only been back one year when she, the devout cradle Catholic, met Scott, who was studying to become a Buddhist monk. Their relationship progressed, and Scott ultimately chose a wedding band over a monk's robe. After they married, Scott earned a degree in soil microbiology from LSU, and the young couple eventually produced two great children. The boy is named Andrew. The girl, who happens to be Caroline's best friend, is named Camille.

Scott and Michelle lived what most people would probably describe as a normal life with only an average number of difficulties – until the fall of 2003.

"There were so many things we were having trouble with in the fall of 2003, both big things and small," said Michelle. "A family member was suing us. Scott was very unhappy with his job. I had prayed for 17 years for Scott to have the desire to enter the Catholic Church, and I was becoming discouraged that there had been no movement in that direction."

Scott had been working for three years on a land-use plan for 2000 acres of waterfront property that their friends, Steve and Linda, owned south of Houma, Louisiana. Scott had conceptualized a unique and ambitious plan for the property, but they were still struggling to find the money.

"And there were so many other problems," said Michelle. "The list is too long to remember. I prayed and I also asked my father to pray for me, like many Catholics pray to saints for intervention. I asked Daddy to ask Jesus to help us with the difficulties we were facing," said Michelle. Then she found the Rosary.

"It was a gold plated Rosary that Mimi gave me when I was a child," said Michelle. "I found it in a small porcelain box that one of the kids had painted, although I don't remember putting it there. Seeing it reminded me that we used to say family Rosary before my dad died.

"Anyway, I started saying the Rosary every day. I would keep it in my pocket when I was really frightened, like when we were in court or if I was having a bad day. It seemed to comfort me when I held it.

"After a while, things began to change. Everything I prayed for seemed to be answered in God's way. Against all odds – because the other side had misrepresented so many issues – we won the lawsuit that had been brought against us. We started going to church at Christ the King on the LSU campus, and Scott loved it and decided to go through RCIA there in preparation for becoming a Catholic. A headhunter contacted Scott about a company that eventually offered him a job. Andrew got into cotillion, despite the fact that there was only one opening for an 8th grade boy in the entire city.

"I also prayed for things that didn't seem to be answered, but were later. One of those was my very ill neighbor, for whom others and I were praying, who was eventually healed.

In addition to all of this, Michelle was overwhelmed when Scott found an investor who was willing to put up $5 million to finance the land development project.

"We were absolutely thrilled," said Michelle. "Scott had invested so much time on that project over the three years, sometimes consulting Steve and Linda on a daily basis in order to tweak the plan, and we were ecstatic that we were finally going to get the big commission they had promised."

Michelle catered the reception at Christ the King the night of Scott's Confirmation – one of the most important nights of her life. Although she was exhausted, seeing her husband enter into the full communion of the Catholic Church – the thing she wanted most in the world – was exhilarating.

Although Michelle knew the land deal was presenting some problems, it wasn't until the next day – because he didn't want to ruin the night for her – that Scott told Michelle that the whole land development deal was falling through. Steve and Linda had decided that, despite Scott's years of consulting them, they didn't want to pay him a commission. They said they had changed their minds, and began to behave in a way that Scott and Michelle had never seen in their years of dealing with the couple. Greed seemed to overtake them.

"I was devastated," said Michelle. "All of our dreams of family camps and a retreat house on that beautiful waterfront property seemed smashed. My heart was broken."

The next day, Michelle and I took the girls in our Girl Scout troop and their moms to the beach for a three-day stay. Michelle took the Rosary with her and continued to say it every night.

I think that's a point that is too important to just glaze over. A lot of immature Christians would have forgotten about all the other answered prayers and would have been focused on the big one that backfired. God must be so pleased when He sees us push on and continue to act out of faith – even when our hearts are broken and we're just not really sure where He is in the whole process. Michelle's heart was broken. And then there was one more disappointment.

"The last day of the trip, I woke up and my Rosary was broken," said Michelle. "I remember thinking it was like our dreams. Scott and I had so many dreams for that beautiful piece of property, but now all our dreams were broken.

"I put the Rosary in my pocket and we cleaned up and packed. On the way home, I periodically put my hand in my pocket and held the Rosary. I took it out several times to try to fix it, but I soon realized that I couldn't repair it without a tool.

"When we got home, the first thing I did was go out to Scott's workshop to get some needle-nose pliers to fix my Rosary. I took it out of my pocket and could not believe my eyes. It was *fixed*! My Rosary was back together! I was shaking when I went to find Scott and tell him, and then called my mother to tell her. It was a miracle.

"I've been thinking about that lately, since Katrina hit," said Michelle. "I've been thinking about how lucky we are that we don't have that waterfront property, and that we're not in the middle of a huge development when there's so much devastation down there. I'm sure people are not inclined to purchase anything on the waterfront right now.

"I've said the Rosary every day since that fall of 2003," said Michelle. "I said it for our friend Rebecca who was involved in a dreadful automobile accident. The doctors told her family that her brain stem was severed, and they gave the family absolutely no hope that she would ever recover her neurological function."

The doctors were so confident of their evaluation of Rebecca's condition that the family actually had to enlist their minister to intervene in order to prevent the hospital from harvesting her organs for transplantation.

"I went to the hospital with Scott and Trey, a friend from Scott's office who is a very holy person," said Michelle. "Rebecca had been in a coma for two weeks. The three of us prayed over her, and it was the next morning that she started coming out of her coma."

Michelle not only prays for other people, but she's also been involved in my favorite activity – being used by God to answer another person's prayer.

She told me that she was running errands recently when she spotted a printer/scanner/copier at Sam's that was on closeout. Since Scott needed one for his office, she bought it and took it home. Later that afternoon, she was languishing in a slow-moving checkout line at Wal Mart behind a middle-aged woman who looked sad.

"All she had in her cart was a printer/scanner/copier that looked exactly like the one we had just bought on closeout at Sam's," said Michelle. "I stood there with my basket, wondering if she would think I was some kind of nut if I said something. But I felt such a strong urge. I had to say something."

Finally, Michelle asked the woman if she would mind telling her how much she was paying for the piece of equipment.

"I immediately realized that she might think I was trying to sell her one or something," said Michelle. "But she just looked at me and said, 'Ninety-six dollars. Can you believe it?!' I asked her if she had a Sam's card, and she said she did. I told her I thought we had just bought the same machine at Sam's in the reduced section for $44.

"Then the woman looked at me and said, 'You must be a Christian.' I said, 'Yes, I am. Why?' She said, 'Because I was just standing here praying to God to help me afford this printer, because I need it so bad.' I laughed and said, 'God hears us, doesn't He?' She said, 'Yes, He does.' With that, the woman turned her basket to the side, thanked me twice, and walked off to go to Sam's."

We never know who is going to cross our path in need of help. And we don't ever know when the walls of life might come tumbling down. But God is constant, and He is willing to intervene in every life in the same way that He intervenes in Michelle's. I like the way it's said in the old standard in the Baptist hymnal, "What a Friend We Have in Jesus." (words, Joseph Scriven, 1855. Tune CONVERSE, Charles C. Converse, 1868.)

> What a friend we have in Jesus,
> All our sins and griefs to bear!
> What a privilege to carry
> Everything to God in prayer!
> Oh, what peace we often forfeit,
> Oh, what needless pain we bear,
> All because we do not carry
> Everything to God in prayer!

I frequently hear people who are in a tight spot say, "Well, there's nothing else we can do but pray." That makes it sound like prayer is a last resort, or maybe that it's just a little something to keep our minds occupied once we've exhausted all our reliable, human resources. Instead, we should acknowledge prayer as the first and most effective weapon in our spiritual arsenal.

Michelle has learned that lesson. Her willingness to run to God when she needs help has turned her into a true child of ultimate privilege – a dependant child of the living God.

Chapter 15

Rescue the Perishing

If any of you lacks wisdom, he should ask God, who gives generously to all without finding fault, and it will be given to him. (James 1:5 NIV)

I had prayed for several weeks that the Lord would show me how we should pray for my dear friend Susan's husband, David. I expected an answer. But, as usual, the Lord still managed to surprise me.

I had been drawn into the fray at Susan's request. She was more convinced every day that David's low self-esteem was hindering him in almost every private and professional area of his life.

Like most of us, David was born to young parents whose entire body of knowledge about child rearing could be carved on the head of the proverbial pin. They each had a hair-trigger temper and, like most people in their 20s, were self-absorbed. They were wealthy business people who owned a chain of highly successful restaurants across the South. The father was a sharply dressed, good looking, womanizing, two-fisted drinker. The mother was a vain, self-centered woman who lacked maternal instincts and frequently abandoned her children with sitters in order to join in the merriment that usually surrounded her carousing husband. In their defense, I hasten to add that they would probably be the first to acknowledge that they would do a lot of things differently if they could relive those years.

It was into that less-than-perfect family that ADHD David was born – the youngest of three children and the only artist in the clan. The explosive environment provided by his volatile parents – who punctuated noisy arguments by slinging food, upending tables and brandishing guns – would shape his tender psyche and produce scars that were deeper and more damaging because of his sensitive nature. This chaotic atmosphere, combined with a general attitude of the glorification of business acumen and a disdain for any sort of artistic talent, produced a very difficult atmosphere in which this young violinist was expected to thrive.

As with many artists, David was a man of extremes, and he was true to that nature when it came to his relationship with his family. During a period of estrangement from his parents that lasted for a number of years when he was in his 20s, David landed in some pretty serious financial trouble. When his parents were told about the problem, which had developed through no fault of David's, they sought out their wayward son and produced a high six-figure check that caused his problems to evaporate. The result was that David reestablished a relationship with his parents and flipped from estrangement into such intense gratitude that he moved into absolute denial that his parents had ever done anything wrong. As we all know, a high six-figure check can be a very powerful thing.

David's only avenue under the new set of circumstances, at least in his mind, was to blame his tumultuous past on himself for having been bad. And Susan and I believed that his poor self-image was, at least in part, connected to that self-condemnation.

The problem with denial and self-condemnation in this particular kind of situation is that they look so much like forgiveness. And we all know that forgiveness is such a good thing. However, my personal experience has taught me that the recognition of blame has to come first. Once everyone's slice of responsibility, sized appropriately, has been designated, then everyone can be forgiven and everyone can move on. But that middle stage between anger and forgiveness, the stage of assigning responsibility, can't be skipped. If it is, an important link in the chain will be missing, and it can sometimes cause problems like the ones we were seeing in David.

It only took a couple of conversations with David to recognize that he was absolutely committed to holding the line on denial. He was unwilling to go back into any of that painful past to the extent that would be necessary in order to process what had happened or to deflect any of the responsibility away from himself. It was easier for him to continue to believe that he was bad, and that he had brought bad things on himself. And he absolutely refused to consider that he might need professional help.

Stumped, I began to pray that God would show Susan and me how to pray for David.

About a week into this prayer, my Bible study met for the last time before we would break for the Christmas holiday. We gathered in the sanctuary to sing the traditional two songs before the lecture. Old timers had told me that our lecture leader took the selection of the hymns very seriously, and that she prayed over them. I believed it. I'd never heard most of the songs she selected. There were times when she'd have to stop us and start over because everyone was valiantly but unsuccessfully struggling with some obscure melody of a song that was chosen because it had the perfect words.

So, I was delighted to see that her final selection on that last day before the holiday was an old familiar song. It was "Rescue the Perishing." I'd sung that song a bazillion times. But this time the Lord would use it to speak to me in a way that I could never have anticipated.

We sang the first verse, then the second. Then, as we sang the third verse, my breath stopped and I felt my spirit become very alert. I could barely hear the other women as they continued with the fourth verse of the song. I had gone back to reread the verse we had just finished.

"Down in the human heart,
Crush'd by the tempter,
Feelings lie buried that grace can restore;
Touch'd by a loving heart,
Waken'd by kindness,
Chords that are broken will vibrate once more."
(Words, Fanny J. Crosby, 1869. Tune RESCUE, William H. Doane, 1869)

Sweet Jesus. That was it. That was the prayer. I knew that the Holy Spirit was telling me that Susan and I should pray for God to restore the crushed feelings that lay buried in David's heart so that the chords that were broken in her violinist husband's heart would vibrate once more.

We began that prayer. And in only one month, the changes in David were noticeable. Susan confirmed that his harshness had softened, and that he wasn't as hard on her or the kids. He had even apologized to her about a misunderstanding – something that he had never done before.

Several years have passed since that prayer, and David continues to exhibit a mellowing that I describe as becoming more comfortable in his own skin. Like the rest of us, he will never be perfect. But he's growing and moving forward in a way that is such a positive testimony to God's grace.

How to pray for someone can be a challenge. I believe that our first obligation in many cases is to pray for God's wisdom about how to pray for one another. I can honestly say that every time I've done that, the answer has been a surprise.

God loves us. That's a big revelation for a lot of people to get their arms around. Also, He wants to help us. I know it doesn't always look like that to our little finite minds. But it's true. And, if we pray and wait for His guidance, sometimes He'll give us specific directions about how to pray for one another in the most effective way – in a way that we never would have figured out on our own.

Chapter 16

Ms. Mary's Special Day

Yet the Lord longs to be gracious to you; he rises to show you
compassion. (Isaiah 30:18a)

It was one of those drenching South Louisiana rains that you just
knew was going to last for a while. The sky was overcast and the
rain was slow and steady, like it was in absolutely no hurry to finish
the job. And I wondered why, though we needed rain so badly, did it
have to come on Ms. Mary's special day.

Ms. Mary and her daughter, Geri, were the newest residents
in our little neighborhood of only 13 homes. The daughter was a

retired psychologist who had moved back from California to live with and care for her mother. Not that Ms. Mary needed a lot of care. She looked younger than her 88 years, especially when she was out watering her camellias and roses and waving like a young girl to the neighbors as they passed her house.

The local newspaper had run a nice article a few days earlier about Ms. Mary's plans for her 30th St. Joseph's alter, a tradition among South Louisiana Catholics. A convert to Catholicism, Ms. Mary had, according to the article, joined in agreement with her Baptist carpenter that the weather would be good. That's why they had decided to build the alter in the yard instead of on the back porch.

The odds had been in their favor. It had not rained here for several weeks, and the ground was unusually parched for this region. But here it was, almost 2 p.m., the designated starting time for the celebration that was scheduled to last until 4 p.m., and the rain was infuriatingly steady.

"Lord, please," I began to pray. "You know I don't believe in praying about the weather. Half the time, one person is praying for rain to come while another is praying that it will go away. But, Lord, you know how important this is to her. She and her little old carpenter put the alter in the back yard and made such an issue in the paper about how it wasn't going to rain. Surely, Lord, surely there is something you can do."

I turned to Lynn and Caroline and said, "OK. Let's go. Y'all get the umbrellas and let's walk over."

The priest was already there when we arrived. Standing on the back porch, he blessed the fava beans that would eventually be passed out to the guests who were crowded in the house and on the porch in order to stay dry. He looked up and smiled when he saw us, then continued the ceremony. When he finished his part, the priest turned to Ms. Mary and said, "Ms. Mary, would you like to say a few words?"

The quiet, diminutive woman with skin the color of rich peanut butter stepped forward and, in her soft, gentle voice, began to express her thanks to St. Joseph for his help through some hard times over the past years. And, if I had not been there to see it with my own eyes, I would never have believed what happened next.

As Ms. Mary continued to speak to her friends, the slow, drizzling rain stopped, the thick, gray clouds parted, and the sun began to shine down on our little group in all its glory. Ms. Mary never even paused as she thanked all her friends for coming. It was almost as though she had expected the sun to show up at the most dramatic moment in the presentation.

The sun continued to shine as the people visited with one another and enjoyed the food and made donations to Ms. Mary's favorite charity. The crowd was fairly large, so we were delighted to be able to spill out of the house and enjoy the beautiful weather. Lynn and Caroline and I stayed until 3:30, then said our goodbyes and walked home.

As soon as we got home, we all changed clothes and chatted for a few minutes about our plans for the rest of the afternoon and evening. Then I walked back to the front window to see how many people were still at Ms. Mary's party. For the second time that day, I had trouble believing my eyes.

In just the short time since we had arrived home, the sky had once again become overcast and a steady rain was falling. I turned to look at the clock. It was exactly 4 p.m. – the appointed time for Ms. Mary's party to end.

Geri later told me that she got calls from several people over the next few days who said they decided at the last minute not to attend the celebration because it was raining so hard all across the city. "I just told them I didn't know what they were talking about," said Geri, with a big smile. "The sun was shining at our house!"

Ms. Mary outlived her adored daughter. Geri was confined to her bed at home for quite some time due to a terminal illness. I got the call a few moments after she went home to be with the Lord. The appropriate authorities had been called and were on their way, and I awaited their arrival at the house with Ms. Mary and the caregiver and another of our neighbors.

While we waited, we prayed over Geri. I began the prayer, not knowing whether Ms. Mary might find it too challenging in this initial moment of grief. But I had only prayed a few sentences when I heard Ms. Mary take over in her tender voice. The prayer she prayed that day for her darling daughter was one of the most beautiful I've ever heard. It wasn't the wailing prayer of a mother consumed with grief. It was the prayer of a loving mother who was gently placing her precious child in the heavenly Father's arms, grateful that He was there to make certain that her child would never feel another moment of pain.

Ms. Mary doesn't live in that house anymore. She has gone on to heaven to be with her precious daughter and her precious Lord. But her memory still lives there. Every time I look across the street, I can see Ms. Mary standing in the front yard by her rose bushes, waving to the neighbors as they drive past. And seeing her there reminds me of that long-ago day that she stood in her back yard, speaking to a large gathering of her devoted friends, as the Lord parted the clouds and caused the sun to shine down on her dear little head.

Chapter 17

Fear and the Art of Snake Handling

I waited patiently for God to help me; then he listened and heard my cry.
(Psalms 40:1 TLB)

Caroline was developing a fear of snakes, and I was devastated. I realize that the normal mother would be perfectly content for her daughter to be afraid of snakes. But I confess that I am not a normal mother.

My father is the primary reason for my strong feelings about man's relationship with nature. Daddy spent most of his childhood deep in the woods, playing beside creeks with snakes and spiders and all sorts of life forms that would terrify most city slickers. As a child, I remember him coming home in the evening with snapping turtles and tarantulas and other cool creatures that he knew we kids would be thrilled to see. He didn't want us to be afraid of them, but he also taught us a healthy respect. I understood that most had to be handled with care – preferably by someone as experienced as my father.

I remember that one night, when I was 10 or 11 years old and we lived in the country, I turned my bed covers back and discovered a scorpion sleeping comfortably between the sheets. I didn't touch it. I just carefully returned the covers and went to get Daddy. Then I stood by and watched the expert calmly deal with the scorpion.

His attitude about weather was also relaxed. I was blessed to be reared in a home where neither parent was afraid of storms. Consequently, I grew up with no irrational fears about weather. In fact, I only personally know about two times that Daddy felt anxiety about anything. Once was when he was on a gurney in the emergency room, waiting to be told whether his fall from the roof had broken his back. The other time, according to a story he told me, happened when he was serving in the Pacific during World War II.

Daddy was part of the occupation forces that moved from New Guinea into Tokyo immediately after the bombs were dropped on Hiroshima and Nagasaki. One day while there, he heard that one of his cousins was on a tanker anchored in the port in Tokyo. Daddy was from a very close family – most of them lived on adjoining farms – and it was difficult for him that he hadn't spoken to anyone back home in over three years. So he decided to make his way out to the ship for a visit with his kinfolk.

He said he traveled through Tokyo alone, dressed in his United States Army private's uniform. At some point before he reached the dock, this young Louisiana farm boy, barely out of his teens, encountered approximately 12 Imperial Marines, still dressed in their military garb, and all taller than his ample 6'frame. Daddy said he remembered feeling uneasy as he walked past those enemy soldiers who stood silently staring at him.

Nothing at Saline High School in the sand hills of North Louisiana could have prepared him for that.

Not only was Daddy not usually a fearful person himself, but I also learned that he was the one to run to any time my own anxiety threatened to turn into full-blown, knee-knocking panic. I remember when, at the age of twenty-something, I was scheduled to have my wisdom teeth surgically removed in Dallas. A group of well-meaning people with noble motives had convinced me, normally a fearless person myself, that I should be worried. And so I was.

I was in Shreveport the weekend before my scheduled surgery, driving from place to place while I fretted. When I got back to my parents' house, Daddy was sitting on the front porch. I got out of the car, walked up to him, and blurted out, "You've got to help me! I'm scared about having my wisdom teeth removed!"

He lowered his chin and furrowed his brow and, with a tone of disbelief, said, "Sandy! Your wisdom teeth?!!" Then he just sat there, grinning at me. Like warm, free-flowing liquid oozing out of my pores, every ounce of fear instantly drained from my body.

And so it was in the atmosphere of the absence of fear, created by this man, that I grew up. And that's what I wanted for my daughter.

Alas. What we want is not always to be.

Despite my protest, well-meaning people with noble motives had decided that stern warnings about danger were the surest form of protection. Since lakes surround our subdivision, the warnings were often about snakes. And the result was that Caroline was developing a fear of snakes.

I knew Daddy was the solution to that problem. I knew he could turn her around and replace the fear with a healthy respect. But he lived 250 miles away, and it seemed unlikely that a snake would present itself at just the right moment during one of our infrequent visits.

For whatever reason, I've never hesitated to ask for God's help – no matter how large or small the problem. Some people tend to only go to God when the problem is insurmountable. I, on the other hand, have always believed that He doesn't mind getting involved with what some people might consider to be the insignificant details. So I prayed and asked God to help me with this.

I confided my concern to Daddy one weekend when he and Mother were in Baton Rouge for their annual visit. He completely understood, and promised to do what he could if the opportunity arose. But we agreed that the chances were slim that a snake would show up at a convenient moment.

That same afternoon, following the big Grandparents' Day celebration at Caroline's school, Caroline decided she and Mother needed to do some trimming with my new gardening clippers. We had recently gotten a nice rain, and the pale, tender, new growth on the shrubs was a tempting target for a seven-year-old armed with shears.

The two buddies amassed quite a pile of leaves, so I decided to sweep up the greenery. While Daddy watched the fun, I gathered my leaves and took them to the side yard to deposit them into my compost bin.

Now, I'd had that compost bin for two years, and I'd added food scraps or yard clippings almost every day. In all that time, I had never seen anything in the bin except compost. But this time, as I raised the lid, there was a surprise. Coiled right on top of the compost was a 12-inch brown snake that just sat calmly gazing back at me.

I couldn't believe it. And so, just as I had put the covers back over the scorpion in my bed 30 years earlier, I carefully returned the lid to the compost bin and ran to get Daddy.

"You won't believe this," I said to him. "I found a snake!"

Daddy quickly followed me to the compost bin and grabbed the snake's tail just as it was about to disappear into the compost. "You're sure it was solid brown?" he asked, hoping he wasn't pulling out something that would promptly inject him with venom and send him to the emergency room. I was sure, so the gentle pull continued. It took a few minutes, but he was soon able to free the reluctant reptile. I was elated! We had our snake!

When he first took it to show Caroline, she wouldn't touch any part of the snake. But as she watched Daddy calmly handle the slim brown reptile and listened to his quiet reassurance that this was a harmless garden snake, she decided she wanted to know how it felt. As she got more comfortable, Daddy would gently encourage her to hold the head. When she hesitated, he would patiently wait for a while longer, and then ask again if she wanted to hold the snake by herself.

This process went on for about 20 minutes, and then she took the snake into her own two hands. Immediately, I saw her swell with the sweet sense of victory. She played with that snake for another 20 minutes or so, and only reluctantly consented to return it to the compost bin after we had taken a number of pictures for her to show her friends.

That was eight years ago at this writing. I still go to my compost bin almost every day, and I have never seen another snake. Some people might say it was coincidence that the only snake I've ever seen in my compost bin appeared on the day that my father, who only comes to my city once a year, happened to be available.

What I say is that nothing we care about is so small that God isn't willing to get involved.

Chapter 18

Travel Trouble in Texas

God is our refuge and strength, a very present help in trouble.
(Psalms 41:1)

Lynn and I were in our 40s when we married, and had both traveled extensively. I used to laughingly tell people that we had both been everywhere – *twice* – and that we weren't interested in going again. It would probably have been difficult for anyone to put together a trip so fabulous that it could have enticed us to voluntarily leave Louisiana. Years of traveling wherever and whenever we wanted just for fun, and for business – schlepping our luggage through airports and waking up in dark hotel rooms, momentarily uncertain what city we're in – had given us that attitude.

But, once Caroline got old enough to travel, my attitude changed. I was very interested in showing her some of my favorite places. Even that didn't motivate Lynn. He had a lot of music projects and not much time to work on them, so he still wasn't inclined to travel – except for the annual family trip to the beach. Fortunately, I'm confident on my own. Give me a map and I can find my way. Some of the most wonderful times I've had in my entire life have been when Caroline and I were traveling together, just the two of us.

Caroline and I were also blessed with a mother/daughter group that we went places with for several years. Caroline and all the girls she became friends with in pre K and kindergarten just gravitated to one another with absolutely no input from their moms. The moms fell in line with the girls, recognizing that we would need to become a group because our daughters had become a group, and I still find it amazing that the moms all liked one another right from the beginning. We were very involved with our girls. We took them camping many times and they marched in parades and sold Girl Scout cookies and served food to the homeless and we went fishing together and adopted underprivileged families at Christmas and took three-day trips to the beach. Once we even went on a cruise together.

One of the mothers was a widow, one was divorced, and the rest of us were married to men who would go with us if we needed them, but were thrilled if we didn't. So we often took mother/daughter trips. And the day came when some of us decided to take our girls to Cozumel.

The kids were pumped! This was the first time some of them had been out of the country. The trip morphed into a mother/child excursion because we decided to let two of the moms take their sons. The addition of boys provided a more grownup feel. All things considered, this was shaping up to be the trip of a lifetime for our girls.

We booked flights out of Houston, and the plan was to drive there to spend the night before our very early morning flight into Cozumel. My passport had expired, but I didn't have time to have it renewed. I wasn't concerned because I knew we didn't need one to travel to Mexico. All I needed was a photo ID, and my driver's license would work for that. Caroline just needed a birth certificate, and I took the required notarized letter signed by her dad giving me his permission to take her out of the country. So we were set.

The drive to Houston was what you would expect from two SUVs filled with preteens – loud all the way with them communicating from one vehicle to another via walkie-talkies and cell phones. We had an uneventful trip to Houston – the best kind – and were delighted with the motel. It was near the airport and new and clean – a solid combination as far as I'm concerned. We all got a good night's sleep, and the entire group was dressed and ready when the shuttle picked us up the next morning at 6:00.

We got our bags into the airport, and lined up to have our papers examined before we checked in at the airline counter. The gentleman who was looking at papers was working quickly, but doing a thorough job of going over everything – including the notarized letters that we all had brought from the children's fathers. When he got to Caroline and me, he approved her paperwork. Then he turned to me and took my driver's license. He looked at the license and frowned slightly. Then he looked at me and very matter-of-factly said, "You're not going anywhere."

There are times when someone says something to us that is so outrageous – so unthinkably impossible to consider – that our brains truly cannot process the information. The information just keeps spinning around in our heads, searching for a place to file itself, but there's no match with anything that can even be perceived as within the realm of possibility. Well, this was one of those times. My brain truly was unable to compute. I just stared at the man with my mouth partially open. I guess he had seen that look before, because it didn't deter him at all. He returned my license and said to me, without a trace of sympathy, "Your license is expired."

Dear Lord! What? My what was what? Wait a minute! I'll admit that I'm not so efficient that anyone would hire me as a personal secretary, but I'm pretty good at handling life's most urgent, most fundamental tasks – especially when failure to do so might eventually involve me with law enforcement. I wouldn't have let my license expire! Would I? But I looked at the license he had just handed me, and he was right. The expiration date had passed.

Caroline had heard him say I wasn't going anywhere, and the frozen look of astonishment on my face confirmed to her that something was wrong. At this point, the mother in me kicked in. My primary thought was that I had to find some way to keep this from being a disaster for her.

"Caroline," I began, as I struggled to fight my way out of my mental paralysis. "Baby, Mama can't go."

The tears began immediately. She was, after all, only 11 years old. If loving and involved parents – who are always available, both emotionally and physically – have properly nurtured a child, eleven is about the age when some kids begin to assert their independence to the point that they give the impression that they don't need parents anymore. That is, of course, the false bravado of someone who has never experienced even one second of feeling abandoned or neglected or rejected or inadequate. It's amazing how quickly that attitude dissolves when it appears that the dependable parent is not going to be around as anticipated.

Like most parents who adore their children, I wanted to stop the tears. I wanted a letter to suddenly arrive from the Mexican Consulate stating the magic words that would fix this. Unfortunately, I realized there was no possibility of that happening. I was convinced that the only option I had at that point was to do whatever it took to change Caroline's attitude – to convince her that it would be fun for her to go with the group, but without me.

"Caroline, Mama will be fine," I began. "Aunt Louise lives in Conroe, which is just outside of Houston. You can go with the others on the trip, and I'll go stay with her until y'all get back. I'll have fun visiting with Aunt Louise, and you can have fun in Cozumel. Then we can tell each other all about what we did when you get back!" I was trying to make it sound like this could still be a wonderful time for everyone. But it was not working.

"Lord, please," I began praying without even thinking about what I was doing.

Whoa! Hallelujah! I had forgotten to pray – but now my brain had cleared to the point that I was remembering to turn to God! "Lord, help me," I silently begged as I continued to talk to Caroline. "Please help me."

By then, I had two urgent conversations going on at once. One was with my mouth, as I spoke words of comfort to Caroline. The other was going on in my head as I begged God to help me.

"Caroline, you'll have a blast," I said. "You're staying in the room with Michelle and Camille, and you'll be with them every minute. And when you get back, you'll have lots of exciting stories to tell me about all the things y'all did." I simultaneously prayed, "Please, Lord. I need you to help me. I have never felt so helpless. There is absolutely nothing I can do to fix this."

At this point, I turned to the man who had informed me that I wasn't going anywhere. He was busy checking papers for other passengers, and was obviously not interested in taking extra time to discuss my problems with me.

"Please," I said to him. "Is there anyone here who might be able to help me?" He turned and looked toward the airline ticket counter and said, "Go talk to her. She might be able to help."

The woman he directed me toward was just standing behind the counter, waiting for people to begin to check in, and didn't look unusually authoritative in any way that would lead me to believe she would have any answers. I suspected that he had simply directed me toward her because she wasn't busy at the moment and he wanted to get rid of me.

I walked toward the counter, still begging God to help me. As I reached the counter, I held my license out so the woman would be able to look at it as I explained the problem to her. And the moment I held it toward her, just as she touched the license, I clearly felt a voice inside me say, "Look on the back." I say I felt the voice instead of I heard it because – I'm not sure why – it just seems more accurate.

"Look on the back?" I thought. "That makes no sense. Why would I look on the back? We're not discussing organ donation here! I'm trying to go to Mexico!"

But I knew that's what I felt the voice say. So I repeated it to her. "Look on the back," I said. Since I had not yet told her my problem, she had no idea what I was talking about. But, as she turned it over to look on the back, it finally hit me. I remembered that, for the first time ever, I was able to renew my license just six months earlier via the Internet. So, instead of a new license, they had just sent me a renewal sticker. And the sticker was adhered to the back of my license.

I held my hand out to get my license back from the still-confused woman and said, "Thank you. I figured it out, so I don't need your help." She handed me my license, and I stood there briefly, feeling intensely present in that moment, as everything else seemed to fade around me. I whispered, "Thank you, God." And then everything around me came back into my awareness and I went to tell Caroline that everything was OK – that I would be going after all.

Our group had gone on to board the plane, so Caroline and I had a moment to express our relief to one another. I hugged her, and she had time to regain her composure and resume that bravado that had slipped through her fingers earlier.

As we walked toward our plane, I thought about how much I love my daughter, and I recognized that there truly is not a single thing in the world I wouldn't do to help her. But, of all the gifts I've ever given her and of all the things I've ever done for her, she has done something for me that is far greater. She has given me the gift of helping me know how much God loves me. I know that because I know how much I love her. And, because I have experienced that intense love for her, I have grown into the knowledge of how God feels about me.

While I was standing in that airport in Houston, loving my child and trying to figure out a way to help her, God was there beside me, loving me and communicating with me in order to help me. And when it was all over, I hugged her to comfort her, just like I felt that He hugged me to comfort me in that brief time that I felt so present in the moment.

God loves me. It sounds so simple, but it's not. It is overwhelming. He loves me. He loves me even more than I love Caroline. In fact, I'm His favorite child. And the good news is – so are you.

Chapter 19

The Electronic Age and the Word of God

This book of the law shall not depart out of thy mouth; but thou shalt meditate therein day and night, that thou mayest observe to do according to all that is written therein; for then thou shalt make thy way prosperous, and then thou shalt have good success. (Joshua 1:8)

"I know the Ten Commandments," said Lynn. "What else is there?" That's how my husband felt about studying the Bible.

Lynn had grown up in a denomination that, for many centuries, had taught that Bible interpretation was best left to the professionals. The denomination had changed that stance over the years, but it was too late to have any influence on my husband. Consequently, his knowledge of the Bible was – shall we say – limited.

By contrast, I had grown up in a denomination that encouraged its members to read the Bible, study it, and memorize verses. I had also involved myself in Bible studies later in life, and I knew how much I had gotten from studying the lives of the "Heroes of the Faith" and the teachings of Jesus. I wanted that for Lynn, but I wasn't silly enough to think I would be able to say or do anything that would motivate him to become a Bible scholar.

I decided to make this problem a subject of prayer for my prayer group. So, on November 20, I asked them to pray for "…the Lord to give Lynn a hunger for the Word."

Things got hectic, as they do for everyone during that time of year. I continued to pray my prayer for Lynn through preparations for Thanksgiving dinner and then as we put up the Christmas tree. I prayed through the routine of Christmas shopping and then preparations for Christmas dinner.

On Christmas day, we opened our gifts and one of the things my husband gave me was an electronic Bible. Now, with all due respect to the people who make electronic Bibles, I couldn't imagine why I would want one. I already had enough Bibles to open my own Christian bookstore. And I had a concordance. And I had a Bible dictionary. So I wasn't sure why I needed an electronic Bible.

But my electronic-gadget-enthusiast husband was so proud of himself for having thought of this wonderful gift that I just couldn't bring myself to return it to the store. Besides, I reasoned that there might be some special feature that I would just love once I knew about it, so I determined to withhold final judgment until I had a chance to fiddle with it and find out what it would do.

Life remained chaotic until we finally put away all the Christmas decorations shortly after the first of the year. I still hadn't had time to spend with the electronic Bible.

One night, shortly after I had tucked Caroline into bed, I walked into the den and was absolutely astonished to come face to face with a glorious answer to my prayer. There on the sofa, relaxed and deep in concentration, sat my electronic-gadget-enthusiast husband, electronic Bible in hand, intently reading the Word of God.

I was so thrilled I almost laughed out loud. Of course! God knew that Lynn, who is joined at the hip with his computer, uses all the features on his cell phone, only finally stopped obsessing over his Blackberry when his thumbs got sore, and has enough electronic music equipment to stock a recording studio, would be more interested in an electronic Bible than the traditional printed kind.

Since that day, Lynn has read the electronic Bible regularly, uses it to research certain words, and often reads it aloud to me. Once again, God answered one of my prayers in a surprising way – a way that would never have even entered my mind.

If I could give young husbands and wives only one piece of advice, it would be – don't ever try to change your mate. Don't try to argue or nag or cajole or convince or encourage or persuade them in areas where you know they need to do better. Just pray, pray, pray.

My husband probably still wouldn't describe himself as a Bible scholar. But I'm impressed with how often he paraphrases scripture, and how devotedly he follows along in the Word during Sunday services. If I'd done it my way – trying to "encourage" him on my own – he might have dug in his heels and been determined to resist. At best, I would probably still be working on it. But God knew how to capture Lynn's interest. And it was a way that would never have entered my mind.

God knew something I didn't know. He knew what medium would hold Lynn's interest. God knows a bunch of stuff we don't know about every single situation in our lives. He also knows the future. When you just boil it down to that, how hilarious it is for us to embark on any course of action, based on our own plan, without asking His help. When we've made the commitment to walk in the Spirit instead of in the ways of man, God's help is our guarantee of success.

One of my friends in my Bible study, Aimee, came up with a good slogan for people who continue to struggle with trying to nag their mate or their children into compliance. "Shut up and smile!" I would add to that. My suggested slogan is, "Shut up and smile and pray!" Remember – His help is our only guarantee of success.

Chapter 20

My Friend Lourdes

For God hath not given us a spirit of fear, but of power and of love and of a sound mind.
(2 Timothy 1:7)

"I really wasn't afraid," said my friend Lourdes, as she recalls the results of the sonogram that the pediatrician had ordered 14 years earlier. "I could tell the technician was trying not to scare me."

A life of uncertainty had provided Lourdes with a number of opportunities to practice controlling her fear. She was born in Cuba in March of 1958, just nine months before Fidel Castro rose to power. Her godparents, who left shortly before the Bay of Pigs in 1961, were part of the early migration to the United States that lasted until direct immigration was halted after the 1962 Cuban missile crisis.

In late 1965, the Cuban government began allowing people to leave again on "freedom flights" to Miami. In 1966, when Lourdes was only seven years old, her father filed the necessary papers to request permission to take his family out of Cuba on one of those flights. As was the practice, he immediately lost his job and was taken to a labor camp where he would spend the next three years working in the fields for the government. During the time that he was detained, he was only allowed to visit his family every month or so for a few days. Lourdes' mother, who had spent her days as a homemaker and caring for her children, was forced to go to work as a seamstress in order to support the family.

"I would come home from school and Mama would be sewing," said Lourdes. "She would sew until it began to get dark and she couldn't see well. The lights we had there were not as good as what we're accustomed to here. I remember women coming to the house for fittings," she said. "I know money was tight. It cost 50 cents to go to a movie. The movie theater was near us, but we never went. One day a neighbor gave my mother 50 cents so I could go to a movie."

Lourdes remembers the day at school that she refused the red bandana worn by the Pioneers, the youth group formed by Castro. "I told them I couldn't join the group because we were leaving," said Lourdes. "After that, my younger brother and I were sometimes mistreated by the Communists who worked at the school. My principal hated me and would do anything to cause me trouble," she said. "It was stressful, because we knew we didn't dare do anything wrong. We knew we couldn't take a chance that someone would get angry and make trouble for us in order to keep our family from being allowed to leave the country. That's when I learned how to blend in and try to disappear."

When Lourdes' father turned 50, he was allowed to go home to live, but he continued to work for the government. Lourdes' mom continued to sew to support the family.

"I can remember times when we were hungry because there just wasn't enough food," said Lourdes. "Daddy worked at a chicken plant, and sometimes he would bring home eggs. We would share them with the neighbors who could be trusted. There was a policeman who lived across the street. He was more Communist than Castro! We had to be very careful that he didn't see what we were doing.

"Fortunately, Daddy had friends who were farmers. When Daddy was at home, he would stay up at night making chains out of wire for the farmers to use to chain their animals. Then, late at night, he would sneak into the countryside and trade the chains for food. I don't know what we would have done if Daddy didn't have those friendships. I don't know how the people in Havana made it."

Lourdes was at home the day word finally came that the family would be allowed to leave for the United States.

"The government officials came with our papers and told us we would leave in 10 days," she said. "They told us we would be allowed to take only one suitcase full of personal possessions for the entire family, excluding jewelry, and then they immediately began an inventory of the contents of the house. When the inventory was finished, the house was sealed and we were not permitted to go back in. We had to stay with relatives until we left.

"In the rush, Mama had forgotten the money that she had put aside for us to live on for the 10 days. It was still in the house. I remember that it was very frightening when she had to sneak back into the sealed house in order to get the money."

When the day came for them to leave, a cousin took the family to the airport in Varadero. When the plane took off, Lourdes and her family became part of more than half a million Cubans who would flee to the United States until Castro suspended the flights in 1973.

"The flight was a little scary for the ones who had never flown, but everyone was very excited," said Lourdes. "It was like winning the lottery!"

It was cold when the plane landed in Miami that day in February of 1971. "We were immediately taken to the House of Liberty," said Lourdes, "where the U. S. Government gave Daddy $25 and issued sweat suits and winter coats for each of us." Because her godparents lived in Louisiana, Lourdes and her mother and father and brother, with their one little suitcase containing their only worldly possessions, were put on a flight to New Orleans.

"The weather was bad during that flight, and people were afraid," said Lourdes. "Everyone was praying the Rosary.

"When we landed in New Orleans, they took us to an apartment complex in Park Chester. We got settled there, and a couple of days later my brother, Jose, and I walked across an eight-lane highway with four other kids from the apartment to see the Cabrini School where some of our friends were enrolled."

A car hit Jose when they were crossing the highway to go back to the apartment. "They had to take him to the hospital," said Lourdes. "Mama had to take another little boy from the apartment complex with them so he could translate." Fortunately, the x-rays showed that there was just one small cracked bone in Jose's ankle, so they were able to take him home from the hospital that same day.

Lourdes' parents eventually got jobs in Baton Rouge, and enrolled the kids in school. Lourdes went on to earn degrees in both chemical engineering and computer science from Louisiana State University.

Lourdes met Rob, a civil engineering graduate from LSU, and they were married in 1985. They wanted a family, but Lourdes had periodically been on prednisone since she was diagnosed with Crohns in 1977. She was told that one of the side effects of prednisone is the inability to get pregnant. As the Crohns had worsened after the initial diagnoses, Lourdes suffered an intestinal rupture in 1984, and then was back in the hospital in 1986.

In 1988, three years after she and Rob were married, Lourdes heard from some Latin friends who were planning a trip to Medjugorje, a small village in Bosnia-Herzegovina where the Blessed Virgin Mary has been appearing and giving messages to the world since 1981. Lourdes had been given a special Rosary by a friend who had returned from Medjugorje – a Rosary that had turned to gold in color while the friend was there. It piqued her interest, and she talked Rob into making the trip.

"The doctors told me not to go," said Lourdes, "but we signed up for the trip anyway." Then, just two days before they were scheduled to leave, Lourdes got sick.

"I was determined to go," said Lourdes, shaking her head. "I was just determined to go."

And so she did.

I asked Lourdes if she prayed for herself while she was in Medjugorje. Her answer surprised me.

"I really don't remember praying for myself," she said. "I had a list of prayers for others. But I was so caught up in the experience of being there, I didn't even think about myself being sick."

The group she traveled with expressed their amazement that Lourdes did so well during the trip. And there was even more amazement in store for Rob and Lourdes when they got home. Shortly after they got back from Medjugorje, Lourdes went to the doctor and found out that she was pregnant.

The doctors were surprised – and concerned, of course. Her pregnancy was classified as high-risk. Four months into the pregnancy, the doctors were alarmed by the fact that, although she had suffered no flare-ups of her Crohns, she had not gained any weight at all. But, suddenly, in the fifth month of her pregnancy, Lourdes gained weight. By the end of her pregnancy, she had gained 15 pounds and delivered a healthy, full-term, eight-pound boy. They named him Paul.

The doctors cautioned her not to breastfeed because they said she needed to reserve all her resources for herself. "I breastfed anyway," said Lourdes, with a big smile and her black eyes sparkling. "And gained weight!"

Paul was just over two years old when Rob and Lourdes received their second surprise. Paul was going to be a big brother.

Lourdes was, of course, again classified as high-risk. The doctors were determined to follow her closely, as they had before, and scheduled her for a sonogram when she was in her fourth month.

"Soon after the technician started the sonogram, I could see that she was concerned," said Lourdes. "I asked her if she could tell the sex of the baby. She said that she couldn't tell because there wasn't enough amniotic fluid for the baby to move around. I could tell that she was trying not to scare me."

It was the day after the sonogram that Lourdes got a call from Marta.

Marta is a tall, black woman from the area of Cruces, Cuba, where Lourdes lived as a child. Marta also was sent to New Orleans when she left Cuba, and is known to have "the gift." Lourdes had gone to New Orleans to see Marta some years before Paul was born when a friend recommended that Marta might be able to help Lourdes with her depression. Marta prayed for Lourdes, and told her she needed to move to an apartment with a lot of light. Lourdes and Rob moved, and the depression lifted.

After that, Marta had kept in touch with Lourdes. "She would call when she came to Baton Rouge," said Lourdes. "She seemed to know when I needed something even before I did. There are no surprises for her. Maybe for me, but not for Marta. Usually she calls me and tells me she needs to see me."

When Marta called this time, she said she would be in town the next day and wanted to come over. Lourdes told her to come, but said nothing about the sonogram results.

"When Marta walked through the door, she seemed concerned and asked me what was wrong," said Lourdes. "I told her about the sonogram, and she said, 'We need to pray *now*!'"

Marta immediately put Lourdes in the bathtub and began to pour water over her and pray. "She kept praying and pouring water over me and saying that we needed to get more fluid," said Lourdes. "Before she left, she told me to let her know what the doctor said when I went back for the next sonogram."

Several days later, Lourdes went back into the same room with the same technician who had done the first sonogram. The exam began, and once again the technician was visibly shaken. "I remember the look on her face," said Lourdes. "She asked me what I had done differently – whether I had changed my diet. I told her I hadn't done anything differently.

"The technician said, 'I don't understand it. Your fluids are normal.' And she immediately left the room to tell the doctor."

From that moment, except for having to spend the last four months in bed, Lourdes' pregnancy went well. Once again, there was no flare-up of Crohns during her pregnancy. And once again, she delivered a healthy, full-term baby. They named this one Victoria. And Victoria has been one of Caroline's best friends since they were four years old.

If there is ever a contest for poster girl for victory in impossible situations, Lourdes will be my nominee. She has lived her life in a state of uncertainty, overcoming the impossible, often in physical pain. She has lingered in valleys where the average person would have drowned in fear. She suffered with her parents through the great sadness of the sudden death of her precious brother, Jose, with whom she had been through so much, when he was only 42 years old. Yet she has managed to come through the other side of all this difficulty and tragedy with enthusiasm for life, looking forward to what the next day might hold. And she has done it all with dignity and grace, while maintaining a spirit of joy and selflessness and a steadfast trust in God that I think I have not known in many people.

Lourdes' entire life has been a tribute to the power of prayer to rescue us, sustain us and produce miracles in our lives. And I am honored to call her my friend.

Chapter 21

Fishing in California

"Come, follow me," Jesus said, "and I will make you fishers of men."
(Matthew 4:19 NIV)

"California or bust," I whispered, and winked at 11-year-old Caroline as we buckled up and prepared for takeoff.

Like most people, I love California. I've been there a number of times over the years, and had very eagerly waited for Caroline to be old enough for me to introduce her to my favorite part of the state – the magnificent stretch between Big Sur and the Napa Valley. Base camp for our two-week stay would be the home of my dear friends, Martin and Laura, in San Francisco.

Martin and Laura's two teenagers were spending the summer in Europe with their grandparents, so Caroline and I each had our own private bedroom in their wonderful old tri-level northern California home that seemed to become suspended in heaven when the fog rolled in at night. Waking up in the morning was an adventure, a chance to watch the fog burn off so we could confirm that the house was still anchored to the ground. Martin and Laura also very generously offered us the use of their extra car – a fast, bright red compact that was perfect for zipping around the regal mountains and through the busy city streets – so we were excited about the two weeks ahead of us.

Martin and I were friends for a long time before he met Laura. He is *very* German – tall and thin and capable of being quite controlled in his mannerism. He is a warm and kind man. But when he gets irritated, he exhibits that crisp, clipped style that would intimidate the Queen of England. Laura is a petite, dark-haired Spaniard who is delightfully eccentric, passionate about almost everything, highly intellectual, and loves to cook, eat, drink and travel. They sound like an odd couple, but they share many interests and genuinely like and love each other. As is so often the case in these matters, they balance one another and their relationship works beautifully.

Martin and Laura had stayed with Lynn and Caroline and me on a couple of occasions when they visited South Louisiana, and had encouraged us to stay with them when Caroline was ready to visit the Pacific Coast. Although the plan for most of the two weeks was for Caroline and me to do our own thing while using their house as our primary base of operations, Martin had arranged to take off a couple of days and hang out with us. On one of those days, he chauffeured us around to certain historic churches in the city that I wanted to show Caroline. It was at the end of that day that our conversation turned to things spiritual.

Caroline was watching TV, and Martin and I were sitting in the kitchen talking with Laura while she prepared dinner. I don't remember exactly how the conversation turned to Jesus, because it had never happened in the previous years of our long-distance friendship, but I suppose it was prompted by our discussion about how Martin and Caroline and I had spent the day. What I do remember is that things naturally evolved and I found myself telling them about my defining moment at the Francis Schaeffer seminar at SMU 25 years earlier. Halfway into recounting that experience, I could sense that it was not being received particularly well. Martin's reaction seemed to be surprise, with maybe a touch of amusement that thankfully stopped short of condescension. But I actually began to sense tension from Laura, who had spent much of the time with her back turned to us while she worked in the kitchen.

Once I realized that my story was not generating an especially positive reaction, I felt like I needed to end my monologue as gracefully as possible. I considered pretending to faint. In the end, I elected to finish my story, but jumped to the abbreviated version so I could wrap it up quickly.

When I finished, Laura made some remark about Jesus that so startled me that I can't remember exactly what she said. I just remember my reply. I simply said, "When you consider the claims that Jesus made about Himself and the things that He allowed others to believe about Him, I think you have to conclude one of two things. He was either the Son of God or He was insane." To which she quickly replied, "I think He was insane."

It was at that point that many people would have gotten into an argument – which, in my humble opinion, is one reason non-Christians are so put off by Christians. Short of the appearance of Jesus himself in that room at that moment, nothing was going to change anybody's mind. So, I just calmly said, "Well, that's one of the choices."

There was a modest attempt at some mild backpedaling. I think Laura may have realized that she had reacted with a little more intensity than she had intended. But the mindset had been revealed. And I knew what I had to do.

At that moment, I began praying for Martin and Laura. I prayed the prayer that I frequently say for the unsaved or for lukewarm Christians or for people about whom I am simply unsure in terms of their relationship with God. I began praying that the Holy Spirit would draw them toward the light of the truth of Jesus Christ.

About a year and a half passed as I continued to pray that prayer for Martin and Laura. We spoke periodically and emailed regularly. They came and spent a few days with us. On their way back to California, they stopped in Colorado and bought a home that they plan to lease until they retire and move there themselves.

At some point during a phone conversation after they had returned home to San Francisco, Martin and Laura told me that circumstances surrounding the purchase of their retirement home had evolved in such a way that they believed that God had a hand in managing the events. They were both very moved by the way things had unfolded, and they wanted me to know that they had returned to the Church.

That, my dear friend, is a far cry from thinking Jesus is insane.

When I look back on Caroline's first trip to California – which was actually a spur-of-the-moment affair, hurriedly thrown together in less that two weeks – I realize that we weren't there just to see the sites. We were there on a fishing expedition, specifically trusted by God to recognize the situation because He knew I would listen to His prompt and cast the nets in the form of prayer.

If you've ever watched a fisherman cast his net, you've probably noticed that it is a slow, gentle process of gathering that requires both patience and wisdom about where and when and exactly how to cast. When Jesus said He would make us fishers of men, I think that's the method He had in mind. I don't think He intended for us to club the fish to death.

Caroline's first trip to California was delightful, and one of the most memorable times that she and I have ever spent together. But the greatest reward of the trip for me was the privilege of being used by God as a vehicle of prayer to draw two of His wayward children back into the boat.

Chapter 22

Get High with God

So, as the Holy Spirit says: 'Today, if you hear his voice,
do not harden your hearts....'
(Hebrews 3:7-8 NIV)

I've never tried cocaine or heroin or meth or any of those other chemicals that Satan uses to pull us off point – like some poorly trained bird dog – and ruin our lives. But I can't imagine that the high from those drugs can even begin to compare to the high I get when I find out that I've been used by God to answer someone else's prayer in a way that required very precise timing.

One of those times surrounded a young woman at our church named Julie. Although she and her husband had two children and Julie's salary was modest, the couple decided that their future was unacceptably bleak unless the husband prepared himself for a better job. So he went back to school.

I barely knew this couple, but circumstances threw Julie and me together one day for about an hour. During that time, she opened up to me about some of their struggles, many of which revolved around inadequate finances. As she told me about her family, I was moved by the couple's dedication to their children, Julie's support of her husband's educational pursuits, and the young family's devotion to God.

Several weeks passed. I would occasionally see her at church or when we picked our children up at school, but we never had another time of one-on-one contact.

A month or two after my only encounter with Julie, Lynn and I received a couple of unexpected checks in the mail that totaled $5,000. I knew that I needed to tithe on that money. And at some point, I began to feel the urging of the Holy Spirit to give the $500 to Julie. Along with that urging of the Spirit, I also received the impression that the money was to be anonymous. So I determined that I would buy a money order at a convenience store and mail it to her.

A few days passed – maybe a week. I was typically busy, and I just kept forgetting. One day, as I was driving to get my daughter from school, I felt a strong signal that I needed to get the money order that day. I immediately pulled into a convenience store and bought a money order.

I had never purchased a money order, so I was not prepared for what they look like. The paper is flimsy. It reminded me of junk mail. I could just imagine that someone might get that in the mail, think it was the trick of some advertiser, and throw it away. Or, I was concerned that it might get stolen or lost in the mail and I might never know. I decided the best thing for me to do was to take the money order to one of the church staff members and ask them to personally hand the slip of paper to Julie.

So, the following day, I went to one of the older ladies on the staff and she agreed to handle the delivery for me. It wasn't until that dear lady sought me out in church about two weeks later that I found out what happened.

She said she called Julie, told her she had something to give her, and asked her to stop by the office when she could. Julie came in the next day. The dear little saint said that when she handed over the money order, Julie first just sat staring at the paper without saying a word. Then she started to cry. Then she began to sob. She confided that they had been struggling for about a month because they were so desperately in need of money. She said that just the night before, she had gotten on her knees and cried out to God as never before. She said she wept before God, and implored Him to do something to help them. It was the very next morning that she got the call to come to the church.

I later received a precious thank-you note from Julie, sent to me through the same little saint who handled the delivery of the money order. I have just a few thank-you notes that are so special to me that I have kept them in my organizer through the years. And one of those is Julie's.

A more recent and less dramatic case involved an "attaboy." While visiting my niece and her family in Jackson, Tennessee, I read "Let my People Go," a book by Jackson resident Lisa Clements. I enjoyed the book tremendously, and told my niece that I would write Lisa a letter when I got home.

I got busy when we came home, and four or five days passed before I finally remembered to write that letter. Several days after I mailed it to Jackson, I received an email from Lisa. It read, in part, as follows:

"Dear Sandy: Thank you so much for your letter. It came at just the right time. I had prayed that morning and asked God to encourage me concerning the book and then your letter arrived." She closed by saying, "Thanks for the encouragement! You were used by the Lord."

"You were used by the Lord." Of all the accolades life has to offer, is it possible that there could be one that is more rewarding, more satisfying, more exhilarating? How gratifying to know that the Creator of the Universe will select us, communicate with us, and allow us to partner with Him in order to accomplish His purpose in the life of a fellow believer.

God needs us to work with Him – to cooperate with Him. He could, of course, have dropped $500 onto the sidewalk in front of Julie as she ran to get her kids at school. And He could have written Lisa a note and stuck it in her mailbox Himself. But that doesn't seem to be the way He works. Instead, He prompts us to take action. And we get to decide whether we will cooperate with His desires or simply ignore Him and go our own way.

I've heard many people, even Christians, criticize God for allowing people to starve in third-world countries, and I've heard them wonder aloud why He doesn't do something to stop the suffering. God has done something. He has blessed some people in some parts of the world with enough knowledge and money that all needs could be met if only we understood our responsibility to be God's ambassadors on this earth – to share with those who haven't been able to figure out how to make things work on their own. If enough of us cared about helping the starving more than we care about a second home or adding another car to our collection or buying the eighth pair of boot-cut black pants, maybe everyone's needs could be met.

God, in my humble opinion, is probably fine with us having a nice house and a car for each family member and two or three pairs of great looking black pants. But we need to let the excess flow through us instead of getting jammed up in our garages and bank accounts and closets and metal storage houses that we have to build in the back yard because the attic and the basement are full. Ultimately, we're even more blessed than the people to whom we give. That applies, of course, not just to the material. It applies to "attaboys" as well.

A lot of people get hung up on the question of to whom we should give money. I once asked for advice about that issue from a very prominent, very influential man who was responsible for giving away large sums of corporate money to organizations in his community that were recommended by trustworthy individuals. "How do you decide whether the organizations that are recommended to you are truly worthy – whether they're approaching issues in the best and most efficient way," I asked. I'll never forget his reply. He said, "I don't worry about that. I just try to help people."

Lives are changed for the better when we listen to God and follow His leading. What I did for Julie and Lisa doesn't necessarily stack up very favorably next to the work being done by people who are on the ground in Africa, performing the physical tasks necessary to feed all of those precious starving babies we've all seen on TV. But, what we need to do is mail a check to Africa (if we can't go ourselves) and then determine to be sensitive to what God needs us to do to meet the needs of His children who exist within our own sphere.

If we follow God's leading, He'll show us where we need to help. He'll show us who needs money, who needs an "attaboy, and who needs our prayers.

Then, after you've tuned in to God and followed His instructions about meeting the needs of others for a while, write me and let me know who you think experienced the greater high. Was it the recipient – or was it you?

Chapter 23

The Greatest Miracle in My Life

Children are a gift from God; they are his reward. (Psalm 127:3 TLB)

Of all the miracles I've experienced in my life, none can compare to the birth of my daughter, Caroline.

I was well into the planning stage of a month-long trip to the Soviet Union when my doctor announced, to my amazement (and probably his) that I was pregnant for the first time. My first question was, "Can I go to Russia?" My doctor looked a little surprised. I got the distinct impression that he'd never heard that question from a middle-aged, first-time pregnancy patient.

After only a moment of serious reflection, he consented. "Actually," he said, "you'll be there during your fourth month. If there's a best time, that's probably it."

And so I was on a ship going down the Dnieper River, headed from Kiev to Odessa on the Black Sea, the first time I felt my daughter kick. I had been sleeping, but was awakened when the ship slammed into the side of a lock as we were going through a dam. Apparently, it also woke Caroline. Only a few moments later, I felt that unmistakable sensation – like an eyelid twitching deep inside of me – unlike anything I had ever felt before. I could never have known that the tiny thing making that barely perceptible movement inside me would, once outside, affect my life much like an on-going series of earthquakes followed by tsunamis and punctuated by periodic volcanic eruptions.

Before I had a child, I spent very little time thinking about the right way to rear one. If someone had asked me for my take on the issue of parent/child control, I would have said that a parent has control over a child until the day the child turns 18, and then the parent no longer has control. It is, of course, much more complicated than that. The release of control actually begins when they're still toddlers, when they're old enough to say, "No! *Me* do it!" From that time, parent and child begin a delicate and complicated dance.

Initially, the dance resembles a tightly choreographed tango, with each partner gazing lovingly at one another as they execute every move perfectly in unison, only occasionally stepping on one another's toes.

At some point during adolescence, the dance changes to a jitterbug, with the dancers sometimes close to one another, sometimes far apart. As the jitterbug progresses, one dancer pulls away and then spins back, or throws their partner into the air and then miraculously catches them just before they hit the floor.

By the time the child reaches the teenage years, the exchange can sometimes more closely resemble the dance between two boxers in a ring. There's lots of bobbing and weaving and ducking as the two spar for a while, each attempting to minimize the damage inflicted by the other, occasionally locked in one another's arms in an awkward display of affection. Then they periodically retreat to their respective corners to glare at one another and be consoled by their sympathetic friends – all of whom, of course, eagerly reinforce the idea that the guy in the other corner bears all the blame and has absolutely no redeeming qualities

Ultimately, the dance is all about the transfer of power – of control. And the only way to stay fast enough on your feet to last through this age-old ritual and bring the entire process to a desirable conclusion is to pray.

It is at the early point, when the dance of the transfer of power first begins, that the parent's prayers must increase. The number of prayers, I have begun to realize, must increase in direct proportion to the amount of control that is being released.

This realization dawned on me the night my 14-year-old daughter came home and related an incident that had happened to her at a dance given by a classmate at her school. One of the girls at the party – a girl who has made it clear for some years that she does not like my daughter – came up to Caroline and shoved her. She didn't push her down. She just shoved her. That's not a distinction that brings me a great deal of comfort, but I suppose I think it's important to make that point clear. The antagonism the girl was feeling toward Caroline at that particular moment had something to do with a boy. I will spare you the melodramatic details.

Some days later, I was praying in the morning. Of course, I always pray for Caroline. But on this particular morning, I felt a very strong urge to specifically pray for her protection from any mean behavior directed toward her by any of the girls at her school who are known to be unkind.

That afternoon, Caroline told me that the same girl who pushed her at the party had run into her in the cafeteria when Caroline was carrying a lunch tray with a bowl of soup. Caroline managed to step back from her tray, holding it at arm's length, and was able to avoid getting soup on her school uniform. She apologized to the girl, assuming it was an accident, and not wanting the girl to feel awkward about what had happened. Caroline later deduced, based on a comment made by one of this girl's friends, that the collision had been a deliberate attempt to cause Caroline to spill the soup on her uniform.

This was now the second occasion of physical contact initiated by this girl. I found that disturbing. I told Caroline that I would be glad to talk to the girl's mother, but she told me not to do that. She felt – and she was probably correct – that any attempt on my part to intervene would only worsen the situation.

And that's when I realized that my role has shifted as Caroline has grown older and more determined to handle her own issues. My role in this dance is to continue the transfer of power. Now, instead of leading the dance, I'm adjusting to following her lead.

And so, as I struggled with the feeling of helplessness that becomes so familiar to parents as their children grow up and their lives become more complicated, I suddenly remembered that the Holy Spirit had prompted me to pray for Caroline's protection from the slings and arrows of unkind girls on the morning of the day that the cafeteria collision occurred.

That's when I began to understand the new system. If a child in preschool had pushed Caroline or deliberately run into her with intentions to cause her harm, I would have immediately gone to the teacher or the mother of the child and taken care of the problem. But I can't do that any more. Now, unless the behavior becomes serious to the point of becoming dangerous, I have to sit back and let Caroline work it out on her own. But that doesn't mean I'm helpless.

The time I once spent actively involved in managing her life now needs to be spent in prayer. Instead of running to the teacher to request intervention, I need to run to God every day and ask Him to intervene. I need to ask Him to give Caroline the wisdom she needs in order to handle herself properly, and ask Him to send angels to protect her and to assist in any way that might be helpful. I also need to ask Him to give her the wisdom to know when she needs to ask for help.

Another point I can't forget is that, when the adversary is known to me, I need to pray for them, too. The most desirable outcome will always be for a change in the heart of any unfortunate child who, out of whatever feelings of inadequacy and/or insecurity, finds it necessary to lash out with aggressive behavior.

Once a mother, always a mother. When Caroline is 50 years old, I'll still be agonizing over anything that prevents her life from being easy and happy. But it's her life. And, in my more rational moments, I remind myself that the strengthening of my daughter's character will not occur while she's sitting on the sofa eating candy and contentedly watching her favorite TV show. It will be built in the trenches, dealing with the assaults of everyday life.

As Caroline matures, I must be willing to gradually and gracefully relinquish my role as leader in this wonderfully rewarding dance between a mother and child. Comforted by the knowledge that the miracle-working power of Almighty God is available to my sweet Caroline through my prayers, I have to be willing to continue the process of letting go of the most amazing miracle God has ever performed in my life.

Chapter 24

The Devil in the Back Seat

The thief comes only to steal and kill and destroy; I have come that they may have life, and have it to the full. (John 10:10 NIV)

Don't let the devil in the back seat. Before you know it, he'll want to drive. My friend Emily learned that lesson. And the only thing that finally forced him from his power position behind the wheel of her life was prayer.

Emily had been a social drinker off and on for a large portion of her adult life. She didn't drink during the week. Weekdays meant work. But weekends often brought parties with friends, and usually included liquor. That was more or less the way Emily lived her life until she found herself pregnant for the first time.

"I immediately stopped drinking," said Emily. "I never took a single drink of alcohol or coffee or a soft drink during my entire easy pregnancy, and was too busy to even think about returning to parties or drinking after my beautiful, healthy son was born."

Women react differently to having a child. Some think being a mother is fine, but are desperate for the time when they can once again suit up, drop the kid at daycare, and head back to the office. Other new moms are ambivalent about the whole mother thing. But, some women are so transformed by the magnificence of mother-hood that they go into a state of bliss. Emily is of the latter ilk.

"I felt a depth of emotion that I never even knew was possible," said Emily. "It was like something had dug down deep inside of me to a place of more intense love than I knew existed. It was a blissful experience, but the chores associated with motherhood were exhausting. It was 24/7, especially because we didn't live in the same town with either of our families. To make matters worse, I just wasn't comfortable leaving my little miracle with sitters."

Like so many young mothers, Emily lost herself in the daily demands of being a wife and mother and taking care of the periph-eral duties associated with the house and yard and cars, etc. "I loved doing this job, and almost every day I thanked God and my husband that I was able to be a stay-at-home mom," she said. "But the duties were consuming.

"Looking back, I realize that there came a time when I discov-ered that having a couple of drinks in the evening was an easy and convenient stress reliever – a nice mini vacation. I didn't have to pack and I didn't have to disrupt my husband's work or my son's schedule. It was quick and easy and available every day at a moments notice – plus it was something I could do while I continued with my responsibilities."

I suspect there are other people out there who have made this unfortunate discovery.

Eventually, things got out of hand. Two drinks at the cocktail hour sometimes turned into three. There are people who drink three our four drinks every night and don't consider it a problem. But

Emily became convinced that she had slipped into an inordinate attachment to alcohol that was not pleasing to God, and was devastated at the thought that it might cause a breech in her relationship with Him.

"I considered reducing the amount of liquor that I consumed," she said, "but I suspected that I would eventually slide back into a progressively greater quantity. So, I decided the best thing for me to do was just stop drinking.

"So, I quit," she said. "For several days – several times.

"I didn't experience any physical symptoms of withdrawal or anything like that. But drinking had become a part of my routine, and I realized that I had established a habit that was not going to be as easy to break as I had thought.

"So, I announced that we would no longer keep liquor in the house. That worked fine until we had a party, or guests for dinner. There was always liquor left over. I had grown accustomed to those quick and easy periods of escape, and it was difficult to resist the temptation when the vehicle that provided the escape was conveniently at hand."

After wrestling with this on her own for a while, the light finally dawned. Emily realized that she had fallen back into her "I-can-do-this-by-myself-because-I-am-a-strong-person" mode. She was doing this out of love for God, but she was trying to do it without His help.

"And so I prayed," said Emily. "I asked for the help of the Holy Spirit to stop this habit.

"Time passed. I'm not sure how long. But I remember that we went on a two-week camping trip with some friends, and we didn't have any liquor with us.

"As soon as we got back from our trip, I began to feel the urge to get back to painting. I guess spending all that time in nature had inspired me. I hadn't painted since my son was born. I just didn't have time. But I began to reminisce about how much I enjoyed painting – about how painting made me feel like my mind and my spirit had gone to another place, and about how it was such a release for me in many ways."

Most people who are involved in a creative profession can relate to going to that other place. It's a place of enormous pleasure and fulfillment, a place that exists only in the person's head and, when accessed, causes the rest of the world to dissolve into oblivion. And it is a world that creative people can only reach through the utilization of their God-given talent.

"I had put my son in mother's day out three mornings a week," said Emily, "and I decided to make that my time to paint. The mornings when he was away would have been an excellent time to pay bills or run errands or any of the multitudes of things that needed to be done. But I decided to use that time for painting instead. I pulled all of my art supplies out of the closet, and quickly became engrossed in a project that I had visualized some years before. At the time, I didn't really think about the fact that I was not drinking. I was just so involved in working on my current project –or thinking about the next one – that my mind was frequently occupied in that blissful place.

"About three weeks into this, I realized that I just wasn't thinking about drinking anymore. It almost seemed to me that working on my painting and looking at it had replaced drinking as the thing that would take me to a blissful place."

I've analyzed Emily's experience (As you've probably gathered, I do that a lot.) as it relates to the rest of us. As a result of that analysis, two things came to mind. The first is that one of the physical laws of the universe is that nature abhors a vacuum. And that led me to the second thing – an experience that I had very soon after my personal conversion when I was 30 years old.

I was, at the time of that conversion, a person who used colorful language. To put it in more honest terms, I cursed. I didn't use the most awful words, but I had no compunction about launching into the more common curse words that so many in our society find acceptable.

Following my dramatic conversion, I began to read the Bible for great lengths of time every day. Suddenly, after a few weeks of this routine, I realized that I didn't curse any more. It hadn't even occurred to me that cursing was a problem, so I had certainly not been seeking a solution. But now, those expletives just didn't come out of my mouth any more. I eventually analyzed this (of course) and realized that I had filled myself with so much of God's Word that it had forced those terms out of my mind – and, consequently, out of my vocabulary.

I realized that the same thing had happened to Emily. Without knowing what was happening, her sudden return to painting had pushed the drinking out of her life. That passion for painting had replaced the desire to drink. When she tried to do it on her own, she was trying to pull the drinking out. And that, predictably, created a vacuum that ultimately sucked the urge to drink back into her psyche. The Holy Spirit knew that the drinking had to be pushed out by something else in order to avoid creating a vacuum.

None of this will come as news to people who have participated in 12-step recovery groups. There are lots of folks out there who have effectively utilized this same process for more years than I know about. Jesus wouldn't be surprised, either. In Matthew 12:43-45 (TLB) He said, "The evil nation is like a man possessed by a demon. For if the demon leaves, it goes into the deserts for a while, seeking rest but finding none. Then it says, 'I will return to the man I came from.' So it returns and finds the man's heart clean but empty! Then the demon finds seven other spirits more evil than itself, and all enter the man and live in him. And so he is worse off than before."

When we pull the undesirable behavior out by our own might, the behavior is temporarily stifled and all appears to be well – all tidy and clean. I think the professionals refer to it as white-knuckle sobriety. But, something has to fill that void. If it's not filled with something positive, then either the old behavior will be sucked back in or the vacuum will suck in something even more destructive.

Destructive habits were the subject of an interesting interview I saw recently on one of the TV network magazine shows. The host had gotten word that there was a high school in Colorado that was well known for its outstanding students who were rarely, if ever, connected with drug use. So, the show host decided to go interview these kids and find out why.

The answer was shockingly simple. One young woman said, "We're just too busy. Everyone here is involved in so many causes and activities that we don't have time to even think about doing drugs!" I would love to see the survey that tells us what percentage of kids who get into trouble have a lot of unsupervised, unstructured time on their hands.

The only thing I would add is that the activity can't just be busy work. The world is full of overworked people who are addicted – in some cases, trying to sedate themselves so they can continue to do jobs that they hate. The kind of replacement activity I'm talking about has to be somehow connected to God – either in the form of His Word or an activity that is related to our God-given talent and God's purpose for our lives. Or both.

The time that any Christian spends drinking or doing drugs, or thinking about drinking or doing drugs or thinking about the fact that they shouldn't be drinking or doing drugs, is more than just wasted time. It is a pitiful and defeated place for a child of God. The desire to be obedient to God, to give up something that we know isn't pleasing to Him, to invite the Holy Spirit to help us, will enable Him to lead us to a place of creative expression that can be more satisfying than any temporary high of any destructive chemical. What we give up truly does not compare to what we receive.

Not for one second do I want to insult serious addicts by comparing what Emily experienced to what they would have to endure in terms of debilitating withdrawal. For the serious addict, professional help and even medical care may be part of the answer. But the principles remain the same. The Holy Spirit will help you get free.

If you've never struggled with demons in the form of addictive behavior in your own life, let me be the first to congratulate you. You've either made a lifetime of wise choices, or you're just plain lucky. But if Satan has managed to finagle his way into the driver's seat in any area of your life – through addiction to drugs or shopping or rage or over-eating or gambling or pornography or any other behavior from the long list of choices – don't think that's the end of the story. God has come that we may have life, and have it to the full. All we have to do is let Him drive.

Chapter 25

When Things Don't Seem to Work Out

"And we know that all things work together for good for them that love
the Lord, for them that are called according to His purpose."
(Romans 8: 28)

S ometimes, it just doesn't seem to work. Sometimes, no matter
how much you want a particular thing, and no matter how long
and hard you pray and believe, the prayers just seem to bounce off
the ceiling. That has happened to me. My first marriage was my
hardest lesson about this phenomenon.

I was married for almost 20 years to a very nice man. In the interest of his privacy, I won't go into the details about the problems that led to the dissolution of that relationship. Suffice it to say that my prayer partners and I prayed and prayed and believed and stood firm and claimed all the promises – but, ultimately, the marriage ended in the D word. Some might make the case that I simply gave up too soon – that I should have stayed and continued to pray and believe until I saw the result I was praying for, no matter how long it took. I won't argue with that. It may be that I simply was not mature enough as a Christian to see it through to the end.

I do, after all, absolutely believe that God hates divorce. And I think it's a huge mistake to throw away a marriage as casually as many people seem to do these days. Especially if children are involved (they were not in my case), I think the harm is so far reaching that the decision to divorce has to be made with extreme caution and with the understanding that the consequences may simply be too great.

Having said that, I will now say this. As much as God hates divorce, He doesn't throw people away because of it. I am proof of that.

Following the divorce, I had the opportunity to get bitter and complain that God had not answered my prayers. Fortunately, I managed to avoid that. And that may be what enabled God to operate in my life in a different manner. Because I must say that things have worked out in a most delightful way.

I had known Lynn casually for several years, and the time came that we began to date and eventually married. During the years that we've been married, I have gained a very interesting perspective on things.

As I often tell Lynn, everything I have in my life that really matters to me I have because of him. Maybe a more accurate way to state that is to say that everything I have in my life that really matters to me I have because God gave it to me through Lynn. It is through this man that God has given me my marriage, my church, my child, and my home. And those are the things that matter most to me in my life. At the risk of sounding like a line from a bad country song, I truly believe that, despite making some pretty serious wrong turns down some crooked roads in my life, I've ended up right where I'm supposed to be.

So, what are we to deduce from all of this?

First of all, I agree with God that divorce is to be hated and should never be entered into casually, simply because the inevitable hard times come. But God understands everything about our situations. He knows who and why and how and all the details that we can never disclose to anyone else. And it's our job to rest in the knowledge that all things can work together for our good if we love God, trust Him, and diligently strive to obey Him.

Sometimes, when we pray, it's a little like walking down a corridor in a hotel, trying to open each door as we progress, looking for the unlocked door that will lead us into the room that holds our answer. Sometimes we get frustrated because so many of the doors are locked, and we're left in the corridor to experience what I call "hell in the hallway." But then, as we get farther down the hall and open the door to the suite that holds something better than we even hoped for, the system starts to make more sense. Because it is then that we realize that it is precisely because the other doors remained locked that we ended up where God most needed us to be. Sometimes God's "no" is simply intended to force us on down the hall toward the better and more significant "yes."

There's another, slightly different twist on the way that living a life of dependence on God sometimes seems to not work out. Some of the previous chapters of this book illustrate what I have begun to refer to as the "lift 'um up/slap 'um down/pick 'um back up" pattern. It's the pattern that I mention in "Daddy Doesn't Want a Dog," and "His Ways are Higher Than Our Ways." In both of those situations, I observed the following stages as they played themselves out:

A. Despondent, presenting your problem to God.
B. The thrill of seeing clear evidence that your prayer had been answered.
C. The immediate, crushing, demoralizing and disappointing blow associated with realizing that the answer was wrong – the feeling that you were mistaken or misled.

D. The subsequent, thrilling blast into the stratosphere when you come to realize that the answer actually wasn't wrong at all – that it was, in fact, a more appropriate answer in light of God's higher understanding of what was needed in the particular situation.

There are two interesting examples of prominent people who are, at the writing of this book, at point C in this phenomenon. Because they are public figures and the situations are of enormous national significance, they will continue to be discussed in the history books.

The first one is Kathleen Blanco, a woman who was given only a slim chance of being elected governor of Louisiana. She was running against some very strong male candidates, and was dismissed by many people as a lightweight. The political analysis of why and how she won is not complicated, but might bore some readers so I'll skip the details.

Although I don't know Kathleen Blanco well enough to call her my friend, I have sat in the privacy of the living room of her home and listened to her describe the agony that she and her husband, "Coach," went through following the death of one of their sons. I have personally watched her express her sincere gratitude to people who have donated large sums of money to her campaign, but have seen her express an even more intensely heart-felt appreciation when someone says, "I'm praying for you." I know Kathleen to be a woman of such deep faith that I believe she would have walked away from the campaign in a New York minute if she had heard from God that He didn't want her to run for governor.

So, when I read that she had been elected, despite pretty significant odds against her, I just knew that God had put her in office. And I knew that she knew that. And I knew there was elation among her family and supporters. And I knew that she would seek God's face in everything she did.

Fast forward to August 2005. Here comes Hurricane Katrina, followed shortly by Rita. In the aftermath, Governor Kathleen Blanco was faced with challenges of a magnitude that few public officials in the history of our country have had to confront, and her performance was universally maligned in the media and in private circles.

Only a few weeks after Kathleen's public humiliation, the second woman, Harriet Meirs, entered the public radar. Like most people, I had never heard of Harriet Meirs before she became President George Bush's stealth nominee to replace Sandra Day O'Conner on the Supreme Court. In the days following the announcement of her nomination, a little information began to leak out about her. One thing I heard is that she had experienced a sincere and defining conversion to a higher level in her relationship with Jesus Christ.

So I speculated about what may have gone on in Harriet's mind during the days between the time that the president first approached her with the possibility of her nomination and the day that the nomination was actually announced. What an exciting time that must have been for her. And, if she is as close to the Lord as people have said she is, how grateful she must have been – how absolutely certain she probably was that God had positioned her to be in the right place at the right moment. She must have been certain that it was a blessing straight from God.

Then came the day of the announcement. The name Harriet Meirs was not long out of the president's mouth before the firestorm erupted. The opposition to her nomination became so widespread and so intense that she ultimately withdrew her name from consideration.

Both of these women are currently at Point C on the chart. It remains to be seen how this will play itself out in both their lives. And I don't know what these women are thinking right now. But the average person, in the same position, would surely be wondering how something that they thought was a blessing from God could have gone so terribly awry. They would be wondering if King Lear was right – that we are only as flies to the gods, put here to be batted around for amusement. Lear was, of course, pretty seriously bogged down in his own personal Point C when he made that comment.

Marathon runners call Point C "hitting the wall." That's when you are totally depleted – physically mentally and emotionally – wondering how in God's name you ever let yourself be talked into entering the stupid marathon in the first place because you now absolutely know that you cannot make it even one more step. Experienced runners know that if you push past that wall, your second wind kicks in and the finish line is in your future.

A friend of mine who is a recording artist who lived in Nashville for quite some time has an interesting observation about Point C and the people who make it to the top of the charts in the music business. She says that the most famous singers are not the best singers around. There are always many other singers out there who look as good and sing as well or better that the big stars. But those others don't "make it," in many cases, because they give up when they reach Point C.

It will be interesting to watch how all of this progresses, and to eventually find out whether life will move Kathleen and Harriet from Point C to Point D. The fact that they're living out their spiritual tests on the international stage makes it all so much more painful. But I hope they find comfort in knowing that the heroes of our faith like Abraham and Moses and David are smiling down on them with complete understanding, reflecting on their own time spent languishing at Point C.

In the meantime, since there's really nothing we can do for Kathleen and Harriet except spend a few minutes praying for them, our focus needs to be on our own personal tests. We may not be in the international spotlight, but we, too, are expected to conduct ourselves in a way that will lead us to God's higher purpose for our lives. That means we don't have the luxury of giving up at Point C.

In the end, it all comes down to trust. If we believe that God loves us (He does), and that He wants the best for us (He does), then we can pray according to His Word and ask Him to intervene in our lives and trust Him to do that in the way that leads to the greater good. There comes a time when the most important thing we can do is put it all in God's hands and begin to praise Him for the solution that we can't yet see, but that we know He has already set in motion and that He has carefully and expertly scheduled to arrive at the perfect place at the precisely determined time.

While we're working on that, we might remind ourselves that, ultimately, every experience in life is simply a personal test. People and situations don't just randomly drop into our lives. They are, instead, all specifically designed to present us with opportunities to strengthen ourselves in our weakest areas. The compulsive talker at the office is there to help you develop your patience. The snobby neighbor is there to help you understand how it made people feel all those times that you were dismissive to them, thereby helping you develop in the area of kindness.

At the risk of getting a little too far out of the box, I'd like to mention a theory a friend of mine has that has helped me tremendously. She believes that our souls met in heaven, before we were born, with every other soul that we will encounter in our entire lives. And each soul agreed on what role they would play – chatty co-worker, snobby neighbor, abusive boss, detached parent, annoying sibling, clumsy waiter, etc. Each person presents us with a test that must be passed, and an opportunity for us to turn to God for His help in passing that test so we can move to a higher level in terms of our spiritual development.

My friend's theory might break down if I analyze it too closely, but it has helped me keep things in perspective. It enables me to move through life's inevitable conflicts without taking any of it too personally. I just remind myself that my reaction to the people in my life should not actually be about what a person has done to me or has failed to do for me. Instead, it's about my relationship with God. The way another friend of mine does that is by always picturing Jesus standing between her and the other person as she delivers her response.

A proper response, based on Godly principles, will move me closer to my spiritual goal of becoming more like Christ. And I try to remember that I owe gratitude to all the people in my life – alas, *especially* to the people who are the most difficult. It is from them that I learn my most valuable lessons and from them that I encounter situations that can serve, if I conduct myself the way God instructed me to, as a catalyst to help my character develop into one that is more pleasing to my Lord.

In the final analysis, it's all good – provided that we cling to God and let Him show us the way. Remember. He usually has something higher for us than Point C. Our part in all of this is simply to trust Him and keep moving forward. Even when things don't seem to be working out.

Author Contact Information

Mail

Sandy Ourso
P. O. Box 44393
Baton Rouge, LA 70804-4393

Web Site

www.sandyourso.com

Printed in the United States
56236LVS00007B/175-1011

9 781600 344343